"These wonderful meditations stirred my C
steps in following Jesus were made firmer by walking alongside these
Anabaptist Christ-followers."

RICHARD MOUW, president emeritus and senior professor of faith and public life at
Fuller Seminary and author of *Uncommon Decency*

"These fresh footsteps marking the path of global Anabaptism lead past
desert casinos and fields of ethnic conflict, down the back streets of
Kolkata and tenements of Hong Kong, along ragged migrant trails and
the grounds of martyrdom. The earnest longing: that they might yet follow
in the path of a resurrected Christ."

JONATHAN P. LARSON, author of *Making Friends among the Taliban*

"The devotionals compiled in *Footsteps of Faith* recount the birth, life,
death and resurrection of Jesus through the remarkably vulnerable testimonies of Anabaptists from across the globe. Many devotional collections
can feel generic—this one does not. The joys and challenges of following
Jesus in Germany, Ethiopia, Costa Rica, and beyond come into high
relief through these deeply personal entries. This is a genuinely moving
collection that I will return to repeatedly for encouragement."

ELIZABETH MILLER, director of the Institute for the Study of Global Anabaptism

"*Footsteps of Faith* does not prioritize Western voices, but invites readers
to engage with a global perspective of our faith, centered on the risen
Christ—the same Christ who called Anabaptist followers 500 years ago
and continues to call us today to rise above the tribalism and nationalism
present in our world."

JASON BARNHART, assistant professor of historical theology at Ashland Theological
Seminary and author of *Word-Spirit Communal Revelationalism*

"Encounter Jesus more fully through the eyes of sisters and brothers from around the world. Forty Anabaptist church leaders, men and women from five continents, draw connections between gospel texts about Jesus' ministry and challenging moments in their own personal journeys of faith. Readers will sense the Holy Spirit's work across cultural and geographical boundaries, inviting all to be part of a global movement of Christ-followers."

ANICKA FAST, secretary of the Faith and Life Commission in Mennonite World Conference and visiting researcher at Boston University Center for Global Christianity and Mission

"A unique devotional book that introduces me to forty spiritual friends from around the globe who are taking footsteps with me."

GARETH BRANDT, author of *Radical Roots*

"It is a rare privilege to sit with forty Anabaptist followers of Jesus from twenty-four countries as they reflect on the Jesus story. But here it is. Grab this gem! And then...sit with it. Marinate in it. And be thankful for the diverse family God is assembling from around the world."

JAMES R. KRABILL, chair of the Mission Commission in Mennonite World Conference and adjunct professor at Anabaptist Mennonite Biblical Seminary

"The personal stories will surprise and challenge you while enveloping you in the deep resonance of scriptural understanding through an Anabaptist lens."

JANET PLENERT, representatives coordinator for Mennonite World Conference

FOOTSTEPS *of* FAITH

FOOTSTEPS *of* FAITH

A GLOBAL ANABAPTIST DEVOTIONAL

Edited by

JOHN D. ROTH

Harrisonburg, Virginia

Herald Press
PO Box 866, Harrisonburg, Virginia 22803
www.HeraldPress.com

Library of Congress Cataloging-in-Publication Data
Names: Roth, John D., 1960- editor.
Title: Footsteps of Faith : a Global Anabaptist Devotional / edited by John
 D. Roth.
Description: Harrisonburg, Virginia : Herald Press, [2025]
Identifiers: LCCN 2024055677 (print) | LCCN 2024055678 (ebook) | ISBN
 9781513815169 (paperback) | ISBN 9781513815176 (ebook)
Subjects: LCSH: Anabaptist preaching. | Anabaptists. | Devotional
 calendars.
Classification: LCC BX4935.P74 F66 2025 (print) | LCC BX4935.P74 (ebook)
 | DDC 242/.8043--dc23/eng/20250110
LC record available at https://lccn.loc.gov/2024055677
LC ebook record available at https://lccn.loc.gov/2024055678

VERSA PRESS

Printing generously donated by Versa Press, East Peoria, IL
and Metamora Mennonite Church, Metamora, IL.

FOOTSTEPS OF FAITH
© 2025 by Herald Press, Harrisonburg, Virginia 22803. 800-245-7894. All rights reserved.
Library of Congress Control Number: 2024055677
International Standard Book Number: 978-1-5138-1516-9 (paperback); 978-1-5138-1517-6 (ebook)
Printed in United States of America
Cover: Yuliya Derbisheva / iStock / Getty Images Plus; werbeantrieb / iStock / Getty Images Plus;
 sensationaldesign/ iStock / Getty Images Plus

29 28 27 26 25   10 9 8 7 6 5 4 3 2 1

CONTENTS

11 *Foreword by César García*

15 *Introduction by John D. Roth*

PART 1: THE PROMISE OF A NEW CREATION

20 The Birth of Jesus
LUKE 2:1–20 | *Felix Perez Diener (United States)*

23 The Flight to Egypt . . . and a Sacred Journey with Seniors
MATTHEW 2:13–15 | *Lisa Carr-Pries (Canada)*

27 Jesus in the Temple at Age Twelve
LUKE 2:41–52 | *Tigist Tesfaye Gelagle (Ethiopia)*

31 John the Baptist Identifies Jesus as the Messiah
JOHN 1:19–34 | *Anne-Cathy Graber (France)*

35 Children of God
MATTHEW 3:13–17 | *Doug Klassen (Canada)*

PART 2: ANNOUNCING THE KINGDOM

40 Jesus Is Tested in the Wilderness
LUKE 4:1–13 | *Sue Park-Hur (United States)*

44 The Cleansing of the Temple:
How Do You Respond to an Angry Jesus?
JOHN 2:13–25 | *Linda Dibble (United States)*

48 Jesus Begins to Gather His Followers
JOHN 1:35–51 | *Nelson Martínez Muñoz (Colombia)*

52 As Jesus Walks . . . He Calls Peter, Andrew, James, and John
MATTHEW 4:18–22 | *Jürg Bräker (Switzerland)*

57 Jesus Teaches the Disciples How to Pray
MATTHEW 6:5–15 | *Kari Traoré (Burkina Faso)*

PART 3: THE KINGDOM TAUGHT

62 The Rock: Peter Confesses Jesus Is the Christ
MATTHEW 16:13–20 | *Reinhard Kummer (Austria)*

67 Jesus Encounters the Woman at the Well . . .
and Jesus Encounters Me
JOHN 4:4–30 | *Cindy Alpízar (Costa Rica)*

71 Jesus Teaches the Parable of the Rich Fool
LUKE 12:13–21 | *Gracia Felo (Democratic Republic of the Congo)*

75 Jesus and Zacchaeus: An Encounter of Transforming Love
LUKE 19:1–10 | *Willi Hugo Pérez (Guatamala)*

80 Jesus Teaches About Service and Gives Warnings
MARK 9:33–50 | *Valentina Kunze (Uruguay)*

PART 4: THE KINGDOM LIVED

86 The Touch of Shalom
MARK 8:22–26 | *Cynthia Peacock (India)*

90 Jesus Heals a Demon-Possessed Man
LUKE 8:26–39 | *Desalegn Abebe (Ethiopia)*

94 Jesus Teaches the Parable of the Good Samaritan
LUKE 10:25–37 | *Preshit Rao (India)*

98 Jesus Forgives a Woman Accused of Adultery
JOHN 8:1–11 | *Barbara Hege-Galle (Germany)*

102 Jesus, the Merciful Savior
JOHN 5:1–15 | *Sunoko Lin (Indonesia/United States)*

PART 5: THE UPSIDE-DOWN KINGDOM

108 Leadership is Serving Rather than Being Served
LUKE 22:24–30 | *Nelson Okanya (Kenya/United States)*

112 Jesus Blesses Children
MARK 10:13–16 | *Hyacinth Stevens (United States)*

117 Jesus Announces Good News to the Poor
LUKE 4:16–30 | *Jeremiah Choi (Hong Kong)*

121 Jesus Challenges His Followers to Full Commitment
LUKE 9:57–62 | *Samson Omondi Ongode (Kenya)*

125 Jesus Teaches About the Narrow Way
LUKE 13:22–30 | *Kkot-Ip Bae (South Korea)*

PART 6: ON THE ROAD TO JERUSALEM

130 The Unsettling Message of Jesus
LUKE 12:51–53 | *Vikal Pravin Rao (India)*

134 Jesus' Triumphal Entry into Jerusalem
MARK 11:1–11 | *Atsuhiro Katano (Japan)*

138 Jesus Institutes the Meal of Remembrance
LUKE 22:14–20 | *Sindah Ngulube (Zimbabwe)*

141 Jesus' Farewell to His Disciples
JOHN 14:1–16:33 | *Wieteke van der Molen (Netherlands)*

145 Jesus Is Crucified
MARK 15:16–39 | *Neal Blough (France)*

PART 7: RESURRECTION

150 Jesus Is Resurrected
MATTHEW 28:1–10 | *Henk Stenvers (Netherlands)*

155 Witnesses to the Resurrection
JOHN 20:1–20 | *Rafael Zaracho (Paraguay)*

160 Jesus Appears to Two on the Road to Emmaus
LUKE 24:13–35 | *Liesa Unger (Germany)*

164 Jesus Appears to Thomas and Other Disciples
JOHN 20:24–29 | *Nelson Martínez Castillo (Colombia)*

168 Jesus Commissions His Disciples to Continue His Work
MARK 16:14–18 | *Rebeca González Torres (Mexico)*

PART 8: NEW LIFE: WALKING IN THE RESURRECTION

174 Jesus Proclaims Good News to the Poor
LUKE 4:14–22 | *Carlos Martínez-García (Mexico)*

179 Jesus Gives the Greatest Commandment
JOHN 15:9–17 | *Mollee Moua (Canada)*

183 Who Do You Say That I Am?
MATTHEW 16:13–20 | *Siaka Traoré (Burkina Faso)*

187 Jesus Sends Out His Disciples to Preach and Heal
LUKE 9:1–6 | *John Wambura (Tanzania)*

191 The Great Commission
MATTHEW 28:16–20 | *Agus W. Mayanto (Indonesia)*

195 *The Contributors*
203 *Notes*
205 *The Editor*

FOREWORD

César García

General Secretary of Mennonite World Conference

*The Word became flesh
and made his home among us.
We have seen his glory,
glory like that of a father's only son,
full of grace and truth.*
—*John 1:14*

The Word became flesh. Jesus lived among humans in a specific time, culture, political reality, and geography. The Jewish world of first-century Palestine provided the framework for his language, ethics, priorities, and relations. This context shaped his life and formed his way of seeing the world. It was in this context that the Word, in the person of Jesus, touched the lives of many people who saw and experienced his glory, grace, and truth. And the incarnation of Jesus allows people of different ages and cultures today to relate with him still today. Led by the Holy Spirit, people from every background, context, and circumstance can still experience his glory, grace, and truth.

Disciples of Jesus have experienced the mystery of the incarnation—the Word made flesh—since the beginning of the church. The experiences of the disciples as recorded in the Gospels were not uniform. They were colored by the context and perspective of each person. A mother's interaction with Jesus differed from that of a tax collector, a Roman soldier, a Jewish fisherman, a widow, or a child. Each perceived Jesus differently. And each was transformed by that encounter in a distinctive way.

All four gospels speak about Jesus, yet each reflects the author's unique perspective and experience. The gospels all emerged out of oral traditions reflecting the wisdom of different communities. They do not all portray Jesus in precisely the same way. Indeed, they reveal among them a theological diversity.

But why do we need four different points of view that give different understandings about Jesus? Why do we have *the Gospels* rather than just one Gospel, the fruit of only one local community? From its beginning, the church regarded unity in diversity as a gift that could help followers of Jesus better understand who Jesus is. A multicultural, interdependent testimony about Jesus, maintained and shaped by different communities, offers a fuller picture of what it means to follow Jesus than we could get from one uniform account. The apostolic church did not rely on only one community's experience (e.g., that of the church in Jerusalem) as the only perspective worthy of consideration. Instead, the testimony about Jesus was consistently multicultural, interdependent, and validated by several communities. We need diversity and multiple experiences to know Jesus better.

As Jesus' disciples today, we are called to build on the testimony of the Gospels and the early church. Personal or isolated experiences with God are not enough. Experiences of a single church in a specific culture may lead us to a partial understanding of Jesus, but it will only be partial since our context shapes our interaction with Jesus and colors our conclusions about Christian discipleship. It is only by listening to others—living in different churches, cultures, and circumstances—and by being attentive to the guidance of the Holy Spirit that we can more fully understand who Jesus is.

That is what makes this book a remarkable project. Here, John D. Roth has solicited a multicultural collection of church leaders throughout the global Anabaptist community to reflect on their own experiences with Jesus. Organized around the life of Jesus, the devotionals gathered in this collection share personal insights and experiences, shaped by specific contexts, that point to the good news proclaimed by Jesus and invite us to transformation.

May God help us hear one another's voices with an open heart. May we learn from the lives of others—their cultures, church, and circumstances, how they have experienced Jesus' glory, grace, and truth—and may we be transformed in that process!

INTRODUCTION

John D. Roth
Editor

When opponents of the Anabaptists of the sixteenth century accused them of heresy, Anabaptists leaders often responded by citing the Apostles' Creed as proof of their orthodoxy. While Balthasar Hubmaier was imprisoned in Zurich in 1526, for example, he wrote a devotional text based almost entirely on the Apostles' Creed. Likewise, Peter Riedemann, an earlier Hutterite leader, drew heavily on the creed for a confession of faith he wrote in the early 1540s.

But the early Anabaptists were never fully comfortable with creedal statements. The practices of daily discipleship, they asserted, mattered more than abstract statements of belief. They also noted how the language of the Apostles' Creed moved directly from Jesus' birth ("born of the virgin Mary") to his death ("suffered under Pontius Pilate"), bypassing entirely any mention of Jesus' teachings or ministry. If, as the Anabaptists believed, Jesus was the fullest revelation of God's character and God's will for humanity, then the details of his life on earth mattered for the Christian life.

The reflections gathered in this devotional are unique for several reasons. First, they focus on the full story of Jesus as presented in the Gospels—not only his birth and death, but also on the good news of the kingdom of God that Jesus announced and taught, the stories of healing that characterized his ministry, the surprising twists of his parables, his embrace of those at the margins, and the abundant life he offered to all who choose to follow in his footsteps. As a devotional that takes readers through the full story of Jesus, *Footsteps of Faith* is a perfect resource for a commemoration of the five hundredth anniversary of Anabaptist beginnings.

This devotional also uniquely highlights perspectives drawn from the global Anabaptist church. Anabaptism emerged in the context of the European Reformation and has found a strong foothold in North America. But during the past fifty years, Anabaptism has profoundly transformed into a truly global movement. In 1975, Anabaptist-related churches around the world comprised roughly 600,000 baptized believers, with the majority living in Europe and North America. Today, the movement numbers more than 2.2 million members, with a significant majority of Anabaptists worshiping in Africa, Asia, and Latin America. By featuring the insights of church leaders from the global Anabaptist church, *Footsteps of Faith* invites you to bear witness to this transformation and to open your mind and heart to fresh perspectives on the gospel story that reflect the rich diversity of the Anabaptist movement today.

In our initial invitation to the forty contributors to this devotional, we asked writers to spend time reflecting on a crucial moment in Jesus' ministry that is recorded in the three synoptic gospels of Matthew, Mark, and Luke. For nearly three years, Jesus had been traveling with the disciples, preaching and teaching, while also healing the sick, restoring broken relationships, and tending to wounded souls. Now, at Caesarea Philippi, he asks the disciples a simple question: "Who do you say that I am?" Simon Peter, of course, gets the answer right:

"You are the Christ, the Son of the Living God" (Matthew 16:15–16). Jesus responds enthusiastically. He names Peter as the "rock," the foundation on which Christ will build the church, granting Peter the "keys of the kingdom of heaven" with the authority to "bind and loose." It is a beautiful moment. Indeed, some Christian traditions have identified this moment as the birthplace of the church.

But the story did not stop with this confession. The real question that remains for the disciples—and for the early church and for us today—is what it means to put this confession into practice. After all, it's relatively easy to say the words "You are the Christ, the Son of the Living God." But how will this confession of faith be expressed in the daily life of believers or in the witness of the gathered church? How will the Word be made flesh?

In this devotional, forty global Anabaptist church leaders seek to answer that question, often in ways that reflect the distinctive realities of their own cultural setting.

As you read the biblical text and personal reflections in each of these devotionals, and as you ponder the reflection questions, do so knowing that you are in conversation with a global community of faith that has been shaped by the legacy of the Anabaptist tradition. But above all, do so with an openness to encounter the living presence of Jesus. May that experience renew and transform you. And may it call you into the world to follow in the footsteps of Jesus the Christ, the Son of the Living God.

Part 1

THE PROMISE OF A NEW CREATION

THE BIRTH OF JESUS

Felix Perez Diener (United States)

LUKE 2:1–20

vv. 6–7 *While they were there, the time came for Mary to have her baby. She gave birth to her firstborn child, a son, wrapped him snugly, and laid him in a manger, because there was no place for them in the guestroom.*

Most days when I wake up, I open my blinds and admire the rocky mountains of the Las Vegas valley. The desert air is thin, and the sunshine feels close to your skin. When I leave for work, I get a good look at the skyscrapers of the Las Vegas Strip. Approximately thirty casinos line this four-mile stretch of road, attracting some forty million visitors to Las Vegas every year. Many of those visitors come hungry for what the casinos promise—instant wealth, a chance to avoid doing things the hard way, the hope of skipping years of work by getting lucky at the tables.

Jesus began his life on earth the hard way, with no shortcuts. In this familiar passage from Luke 2:1–20, we encounter a paradox. Our promised Messiah, the Lord, is born as a baby in a stable. Angels announce his birth to shepherds who travel at night to find him, just as they were told. Jesus, the bright morning star—the one through and for whom creation itself was made—is born of a woman just like you and me. Even more amazing is the fact that he was born in a tiny village to parents of no particular status, and spent the first portion of his life as a refugee in Egypt.

But why start life like an average human being? Why didn't Jesus, the Son of God, simply arrive from heaven fully formed and ready for action?

I believe it is because Jesus' life is characterized by a rejection of shortcuts in the face of difficulty. Early in his ministry he is tempted by Satan to take shortcuts of food, fame, and power. He heals the sick one by one, when he presumably could have just healed everyone at once and gone home. When he hung on the cross, one of the thieves next to him made the easy way out very clear: "Aren't you the Messiah? Save yourself and us!" Yet starting from the circumstances of his birth as a helpless infant, we see Jesus consistently taking the hard path.

The story of Jesus' birth speaks deeply to me, in part, because I love shortcuts. I relish finding new ways to do something quicker and faster. To be honest, in my faith journey I find myself looking for ways to skip steps. Why go through the trouble of reading Scripture and praying? Do I really have to serve others? Why confess sins? God, can't I just be spiritually mature already? Like a gambler in a casino I want to hit the jackpot and skip years of work on the way to becoming a man of God. Reading Luke 2, and thinking of all the challenging circumstances surrounding his birth, I'm reminded again that Jesus didn't skip any steps. Neither should we.

For reflection

1. What shortcuts tempt you the most in your Christian journey? What spiritual disciplines have you come to appreciate, despite risks or investments of time that they required?

2. What stands out to you in a new way as you read this familiar story once again?

Prayer

Lord Jesus, you are the taker of the hard way. We confess we are often tempted to take shortcuts because denying ourselves is hard. Sometimes we even avoid you because we are ashamed to face you; sometimes we fake religious piety. Today we ask you to strengthen our spirits. Help us to rejoice in our trials as they produce steadfastness in us. Make us a people who don't put hope in quick solutions and schemes but always trust in you, the Almighty.

THE FLIGHT TO EGYPT . . . AND A SACRED JOURNEY WITH SENIORS

Lisa Carr-Pries (Canada)

MATTHEW 2:13–15

---

v. 13 *When the magi had departed, an angel from the Lord appeared to Joseph in a dream and said, "Get up. Take the child and his mother and escape to Egypt. Stay there until I tell you, for Herod will soon search for the child in order to kill him."*

In the midst of both the bustle and stillness in the seniors' community where I serve, I encounter the living presence of Jesus on a daily basis. In the deep-hearted hymn singing, the whispers of stories remembered, the buzz of the caregivers, and the glints of joy and fear in the eyes of the residents, I often experience my work here as a profound intersection of the divine and the mundane.

Much like Mary, Joseph, and Jesus embarking on their journey to the unknown place of Egypt, the residents have told me stories about their own paths of fragility and vulnerability. Some have come here not by their own choice but because life circumstances have determined this adventure for them. They come with uncertainty and fear, wondering whether this place will ever feel like home.

As I walk alongside residents, talking or singing with them through laughter and tears, joys and sorrows, I recognize the living presence of Jesus who walks alongside us during our most vulnerable moments.

In the text for today, Herod was searching for Jesus intent on killing him. So an angel warns Jesus and his parents to flee. Forced to run, I can imagine that they hoped to find a refuge in Egypt, a place of sanctuary from the violence and chaos. So many people in our world are in a similar circumstance—longing for peace, belonging, and a place to call home. The seniors in my care are also filled with these deep human longings.

In providing a safe and nurturing place, I and other caregivers try to show Jesus' love, compassion, and understanding for people who are burdened, weary, and sometimes without hope. Through a gentle touch or smile, a prayer of comfort, or an open listening ear, we attempt to be instruments of peace and healing in a world of loneliness and uncertainty.

Despite the fear that must have surrounded their dangerous journey to Egypt, I imagine this small family having quite an adventure. After all, they did have a two-year-old! There must have been occasions of laughter, lots of "Why, mommy?" questions, and a deepening bond as they became a family together. Something similar to this also happens here at the seniors' community. As we share a meal, sing hymns, engage in activities like wheelchair bowling or balloon tennis, or simply sit together at a bedside, we are reminded of Jesus' promise to be with us through all of life's ups and downs. Jesus accompanies us, guides us, supports us, and even has fun with us. In the laughter of family and friends, the shared wisdom of the elderly, and the deep connections that are formed, we catch glimpses of the divine presence that dwells among us.

The experience of accompanying seniors in all of their joys and sorrow has sparked a transformation in my life and faith. I have been shown what deep trust and faith it takes to journey alongside those who are so close to death. Through the vulnerability of aging, the search for home, and the need for community, I see echoes of Joseph, Mary, and Jesus in their own search for home. In the rhythms of life here I have also encountered the living presence of Jesus.

Every day I am surprised anew by the divine as we attune our hearts, minds, and lives to Jesus as our ultimate refuge and our source of hope in a world that needs love, belonging, and healing.

For reflection

1. When in the past have you felt vulnerable or uncertain as you faced the future? Where do you feel most vulnerable or uncertain right now?

2. Who has traveled with you during those times? How did you experience the living presence of Jesus?

3. Who do you know that needs comfort or assurance that they are not alone?

Prayer

Comforting God, reach out and touch us today. May we feel your warm embrace. May your touch give us courage to face the unknowns that are ahead. May the awareness of your presence and love give us comfort and a peace beyond understanding as we all journey towards home.

JESUS IN THE TEMPLE AT AGE TWELVE

Tigist Tesfaye Gelagle (Ethiopia)

LUKE 2:41–52

---

v. 52 *Jesus matured in wisdom and years, and in favor with God and with people.*

In this story of the twelve-year-old Jesus, we encounter a boy visiting the temple for the Passover festival who was hungry to discuss the spiritual and theological questions of his day. Yet this young boy was also deeply connected to God's divine purpose and understanding. He was endowed with wisdom—with a quality of insight that amazed the teachers and all those around them.

Jesus' presence was felt and seen at the temple. He clearly had a deep self-understanding and strong sense of identity and his mission. In his discussion with the teachers—and even in his conversation with his parents—he was focused entirely on God and God's business in the world. Such clarity of understanding, however, came at a cost: prioritizing his mission came at the price of his relationship with his family.

This story—the task to which Jesus was called, the wisdom he acquired, his strong sense of identity, and his relationships with people who cared about him even though they didn't fully understand his message—has implications for our own everyday walk with God.

I live and work in Ethiopia, a country with highly polarized social and political dynamics. The polarization around questions of ethnic identity have especially jeopardized our country's unity. That same polarization has affected the church as well. Clearly, everyone comes from a particular background. But in a country like ours with a long history of mixed ethnic backgrounds, problems emerge if politicians or church leaders openly favor only one ethnic group. This issue becomes especially complicated if one comes from a mixed ethnic background, or if one is born and raised in a metropolitan city where it is very difficult to embrace only one specific ethnic identity. The political dynamic that has created a tension between ethnic groups has also created a tension in my mind, as a struggle over whom to associate with and as an urge to settle on one ethnic group identity. This messy issue in our country has a foot in the church as well.

As Christians who believe that we are children of God and that our primary allegiance is to the kingdom of God, living in such a divided context is not easy. It affects our fellowship, creates challenges in our communication, and threatens our unity. I struggle every day to focus my primary allegiance on Christ, which means regarding my fellow believers as brothers and sisters regardless of their background, language, or ethnicity. The grace to embrace such a view regularly comes from the living presence of Jesus Christ in my life. As I grow deeper in my relationship with God, my desire is to always maintain my conviction to embrace everyone as a brother and sister and as a fellow human being. As I reflect on my own spiritual growth, I recognize that my congregation has played a significant role. My community has helped to nurture spiritual growth through different programs for all age groups, including children and youth ministry. In Bible studies, worship, congregational prayer, and community outreach, my congregation has pursued the kingdom work exemplified by Jesus.

Each moment of our lives is an opportunity to engage with God's purpose. In order to do that, however, we must focus daily on our spiritual growth. I experience the living presence of Jesus through his guidance in my everyday life towards God's will. The maturity in faith that Jesus demonstrated in this passage can inspire us to seek a fuller understanding of God's mission and a deeper commitment to relationship with God. As a follower of Christ, my priority should be on spiritual growth and on cultivating a deeper sense of involvement with God's mission in the world. Jesus' self-confidence and his intimate relationship with God gives me hope and encouragement to strengthen my relationship with God and to develop a deeper sense of self-understanding in light of my calling in this world.

For reflection

1. What might it mean for you to have a deeper relationship with God in your everyday life?

2. How do you sense the living presence of Jesus in your daily life, in your congregation, and in your community? Where do you see God at work in your nation at large?

3. How can you, like Jesus, better focus on kingdom business in your regular life, even in post-Christian contexts?

Prayer

May all those who read this have a continuous dedication to spiritual growth, a heart that is eager for deeper connection with God, and a persistent openness to the mission of the kingdom so that you can feel and enjoy the presence of Jesus in your everyday life. May you be encouraged to cultivate deeper understanding and commitment in your relationship with God, to seek meaning and purpose in your calling, and to be attentive to God's kingdom in all your endeavors whatever your walk of life may be. May the Lord grant you his grace to be bold in sharing the gospel with anyone and not to be ashamed of the one who was not ashamed of us when he died, naked and vulnerable, on the cross. Amen.

JOHN THE BAPTIST IDENTIFIES JESUS AS THE MESSIAH

Anne-Cathy Graber (France)

JOHN 1:19–34

v. 29 *The next day John saw Jesus coming toward him and said, "Look! The Lamb of God who takes away the sin of the world! This is the one about whom I said, 'He who comes after me is really greater than me because he existed before me.'"*

What if John the Baptist has something important to say to the churches of Mennonite World Conference (MWC) as we commemorate the five hundredth anniversary of the beginnings of Anabaptism?

"Who are you? (v. 19, v. 22). This question was repeatedly put to John the Baptist, perhaps because his testimony was so astonishing and disturbing. The same question can be addressed to our worldwide Church. Indeed, we often hear it when we meet with other Christian churches or simply with our neighbors: "Who are you? . . . What do you say about yourself?" (v. 22).

The way in which John the Baptist understands himself could be relevant to our understanding of Anabaptist identity. Note, for example, that in response to the question "Who are you?" John the Baptist gives an unqualified negative reply: "I'm not the Christ. . ." (v. 20); and then, I am not Elijah, not the prophet (v. 21). How strange to begin by presenting oneself in such a negative way! And when he finally responds in the affirmative to say who he really is, John the Baptist borrows someone else's words. He does not use his own words, but those of Isaiah: "I am a voice crying out in the wilderness, make the Lord's path straight . . ." (v. 23). Everything about John the Baptist leaves room for the other and for others. Decentered from himself, he puts Christ and the Word at the center. This is his identity—pointing to someone other than himself.

The question "Why do you baptize if you aren't the Christ, nor Elijah, nor the prophet?" (v. 25), could be understood as: "If you are so insignificant, if you are none of these biblical figures, why do you dare this gesture of baptism?" John the Baptist's interrogators cling to their certainties and their logic—so much so that they have no capacity to see or to welcome Christ. And yet John continues: "Someone greater stands among you, whom you don't recognize" (v. 26). In other words, despite their inability (or even refusal) to know him, Christ remains in the midst of these questioners, not avoiding these uncomfortable places of rejection.

A well-known painting of the crucifixion by Matthias Grünewald portrays John the Baptist in a way that captures this attitude. In the painting, John the Baptist's index finger is disproportionately long, thereby drawing the viewer's attention to someone else (Christ on the cross) and the Word, held in his other hand, is made visible.

The painting even includes the words "He must increase and I must decrease" in discreet lettering.[1]

What if this was the challenge for our churches? Not to put ourselves at the center, not to be self-referential, but to point instead to Christ, the Lamb of God, in order to make his Word heard?

The churches of Mennonite World Conference, like each and every one of us, are not Christ. Nor are we Elijah, or even a prophet. We are not a perfect model of the body of Christ or even perfect examples of humanity or community at its best. But we can choose to be a voice inspired by the One who baptizes in the Holy Spirit—a voice that makes the voiceless among us heard, a voice that proclaims this Good News: "Look, here is the Lamb of God who takes away the sin of the world" (v. 29).

For reflection

1. How do you understand the phrase "Lamb of God" in a context that no longer offers ritual sacrifices?

2. Take some time to look at the artwork by Matthias Grünewald. What strikes you most about this scene?

3. What might it mean for those in the Anabaptist tradition to "decenter" themselves from God's story?

Prayer

God, bless you for sending us your most precious gift, your Son, the Lamb who takes away the sin of the world. Holy Spirit, make us understand what it means to be saved by a lamb who gives his life as a sacrifice for all. And may you, Lamb of God, come and set us free from our false pretensions of omnipotence, which belongs to you alone. May all glory be yours! Amen.

CHILDREN OF GOD

Doug Klassen (Canada)

MATTHEW 3:13–17

---

v. 17 *A voice from heaven said, "This is my Son whom I dearly love; I find happiness in him."*

As I was writing this devotional, I was also packing my suitcase for the Mennonite World Conference Executive Committee meetings in Curitiba, Brazil. Along with clothes for weather much warmer than Winnipeg, Manitoba, where I live, I packed what I always do when I travel—my Bible, personal belongings, files and binders, my computer . . . and my passport.

According to the government of Canada, my passport serves as my identity. When I travel to other countries and go through the immigration and customs process, their request for my passport is a request to learn my identity. Government officials want to see who I am.

In Matthew 3:5 and following we learn that "People from Jerusalem, throughout Judea, and all around the Jordan River came to him

[John the Baptist]." That's a lot of people! How did they know who was who? We know from the birth narratives in Matthew and Luke that people often identified themselves by their hometown. Joseph and Mary went to Bethlehem because "Joseph belonged to David's house and family line." (Luke 2:4). Perhaps those who went to see John the Baptist at the Jordan River traveled as family groups.

However, something interesting happens when Jesus asks for baptism. The scripture tells us, "Heaven was opened to him, and he saw the Spirit of God coming down like a dove and resting on him. A voice from heaven said, 'This is my Son whom I dearly love'" (Matthew 3:16–17). It turns out that there was more to Jesus' identity than just being from the family of David or from the town of Nazareth, where he was currently living (Matthew 2:23). His deepest and truest identity was the Son of God.

It was good that he had that experience in the river. It was good that he heard God's voice naming his identity, because the next few verses describe how Jesus was led into the wilderness to be tempted. There the devil said to him, "If you are the Son of God. . ." (Matthew 4:3 NRSVue)—implying that maybe this was not who he actually was. The devil thought that the most certain way he could pull Jesus away from the heart of God was to have him doubt his identity as the Son of God. People can easily be swayed if they are made to feel like they don't belong.

Despite three attempts to make Jesus doubt his identity in God, Jesus remained steadfast. It seems clear that one reason Jesus was able to do so was because God had called him his Son, his beloved. Unless we have heard God say these words to us, it is much more difficult for us.

Precisely here is where scripture can speak to us. In 1 John 3:1 we read, "See what kind of love the Father has given to us in that we should be called God's children, and that is what we are!"

"And that is what we are" doesn't leave a lot of room for us to doubt. Through the life, death, and resurrection of our Lord and Savior Jesus Christ, we belong to God. Nothing can separate us from that reality (Romans 8:35–39).

What is written on my passport is secondary to what is said about me in scripture. The same is true for you. Beloved, we are God's children now. You belong. Your deepest and truest identity is the fact that through Jesus Christ you have been made a child of God.

For reflection

1. When applying for jobs we often write resumes, identifying ourselves to a future employer. If you were to write a spiritual resume, how would you identify yourself?

2. Which creates the biggest challenge for you to fully embrace: the claim that Jesus is the Son of God or the biblical promise that you are a child of God?

3. List all of the characteristics of God described by the psalmist in Psalm 139.

Prayer

Read Psalm 139 slowly and out loud, claiming each verse as promise that you are a beloved child of God.

Part 2

ANNOUNCING THE KINGDOM

JESUS IS TESTED IN THE WILDERNESS

Sue Park-Hur (United States)

LUKE 4:1–13

v. 1 *Jesus returned from the Jordan River full of the Holy Spirit, and was led by the Spirit into the wilderness. There he was tempted for forty days by the devil.*

This passage takes me back to the small Korean immigrant church in Los Angeles where I grew up. At the end of each year, the church organized a big family Bible quiz. Some of us loved memorizing Bible facts while others didn't see how Bible trivia related to growing in faith. As a competitive child (not very Mennonite!), I recall memorizing the exact order of the temptations Jesus faced in the wilderness: first, he was tempted to turn stones into bread; next, to throw himself from the highest point of the temple; and finally, to bow down to the devil.

As I have grown older, my reading of this passage has evolved. Rather than focusing on the verbs—"turn, throw, bow"—I see that the central question was in the "if" clause. "*If* you are the Son of God. . . ." Satan was trying to get at the question of identity. Do you really think you are the Son of God? How do you know? Why don't you prove it?

Behind the other temptations lies a deeper temptation—namely, to demonstrate that Jesus was who God said he was by a show of power.

In the previous chapter we encounter Jesus being baptized by the Jordan River. It is the definitive moment where heaven opened up, the Spirit of God descended like a dove, and he heard a voice from heaven saying, "This is my beloved Son with whom I am well pleased" (Matthew 3:16–17).

In this moment, God declared Jesus' true identity: Jesus was God's beloved son. This foundational truth of his intimate relationship with God was the basis for Jesus to enter his public ministry. But, just as in the garden of Eden, the tempter immediately questioned what God said: "Did God really say, 'You must not eat from any tree in the garden'?" So it is with us. The tempter makes us question what God has already declared. In so doing, the tempter attacks the heart of our identity—that we are loved and that we belong to God.

As a Korean American woman in ministry, I too have had to do some identity searching. I too have heard the whispering of the evil one saying, "Who do you think you are?" Often, I feel that I need to perform and prove to others that I am worthy of the roles I hold. I know, of course, that I am a child of God; but there still remains a restlessness and a wrestling with the different facets of who I am.

I am ethnically Korean. But since I grew up in the United States, I have often felt disconnected from the history of my ancestors. My passport states that I am a citizen of the United States of America. Nevertheless, I am frequently regarded as a foreigner who gets compliments for speaking good English. I claim my Mennonite identity, but my Asian face and last name do not often match people's perception of what a Mennonite looks like. I am a woman minister in parts of the church where women pastors are still seen as unacceptable. The striving, the need to prove my worth, sometimes gets the best of me.

If I fall into temptation to prove my worth without being rooted in God's unwavering love, I can usually still get the work done, but I have no inner peace. It is only when I focus on my work as rooted in God's unconditional love, and start to see that same belovedness in others, that I trust the power of love to transform my life and those around me.

As I visit Mennonite churches around the country, I also see that many of our faith communities are faced with a similar crisis of collective identity. Who were we and who are we becoming? What makes us distinct in our faith and what needs to be reassessed? These core questions of identity can feel scary and dangerous. But those same questions can also create an opportunity.

The continual work of questioning identity does not need to be a fearful thing if it is done in community. That task provides an opportunity to recenter ourselves, together, in God's unwavering love. We can seek our community for clarity. I have learned that our identity—who we are, and whose we are—is shaped and reshaped in community.

In Luke 4, we see that Jesus, rooted in God's call, does not succumb to the temptation proposed by the devil. Instead of falling into the devil's trap of turning stone into bread, Jesus becomes the Bread of Life. Instead of throwing himself from the temple to prove his power, Jesus becomes the ultimate sacrifice. Instead of acquiring powers of the kingdom through violence and domination, Jesus disarms the powers by choosing to be the prince of peace. Jesus chooses to embrace his identity as God's beloved.

For reflection

1. What part of your identity is easy to embrace? What part of your identity do you have difficulty accepting?

2. When have you felt tempted to prove or perform your worth?

3. Who has helped you to remember that you are God's beloved and that you belong to the Creator?

Prayer

God who has called us beloved, help us stay rooted in that beloved-ness. When we are tempted to prove our worth, help us to remember that we are unshakably yours

THE CLEANSING
OF THE TEMPLE

How Do You Respond to an Angry Jesus?

Linda Dibble (United States)

JOHN 2:13–25

---

v. 15 *He made a whip from ropes and chased them all out of the temple, including the cattle and the sheep. He scattered the coins and overturned the tables of those who exchanged currency.*

What a fascinating scripture passage! I grew up hearing that Jesus is loving, caring, and compassionate. Yet, this passage shows Jesus in a different light—as someone who is authoritative, powerful, and even angry. Even though it may make us uncomfortable, some theologians have suggested that "a theology of anger can help us to construct healthy boundaries. The healthy expression of righteous anger can translate communal despair into compassion-ate action and justice-seeking."[2] Here Jesus is clearly demonstrating righteous anger!

In contrast to the synoptic gospels, where the story of Jesus at the temple appears near the end of Jesus' ministry, John's gospel moves the scene to the beginning of his narrative as a symbolic chal-lenge or to underscore the threat he poses to the existing religious order. John wants his readers to understand who Jesus is—the Son of God—and that he has authority over religious powers.

Chapter two opens with the story of Jesus turning water into wine at a private wedding with family and friends in Cana. Then, as Jesus travels from Cana to Jerusalem to participate in the Jewish Pass-over, the scene shifts and he enters into public space. In Jerusalem, Jesus immediately goes to the temple—the very center of religious authority—where he quickly gains the attention of the Jewish leaders. This is a group that he will continue to contend with throughout the book of John.

At the temple, Jesus witnessed a market exchange where wealthy people bought cattle or sheep for the sacrifices required by the Hebrew scriptures. Poor people, by contrast, had to settle for lowly doves in order to fulfill the requirements of the Law. Jesus has rec-ognized that those in charge of the temple seem to be exploiting and oppressing the poor through high temple taxes and other demands. According to the writer Richard Rohr, "the temple has become totally aligned with King Herod, with the collecting of taxes and money, and the selling of forgiveness."[3] Angry with the abuses inflicted upon those who could not protect themselves, Jesus responds with a dra-matic gesture of overturning tables, scattering coins, and chasing out the moneylenders.

When our systems of injustice inflict harm and abuse upon people and their communities for any reason—greed, race, ethnicity, religion, sexuality, or gender—righteous indignation can be an appropriate response. Anger can move us from complacency to action, speaking out on behalf of those who need protection, love, and acceptance.

When I was in the seventh grade, my family moved from Oregon to rural Mississippi just as desegregation was being introduced into the public schools there. I remember the horror I felt when non-white students were made to sit in the back of the bus or in the back of the classroom. I remember the horrible language some of the teachers and students used to refer to Black students. I remember being ashamed of my whiteness.

Through his teaching and example Jesus makes it clear that I have a responsibility to speak out against the injustices done to others. As I pray for others, Jesus transforms my stony heart to one of compassion and care. Jesus is the reason why I support a refugee fund at my church; he is the reason why I share with organizations such as Mennonite World Conference, Mennonite Central Committee (MCC), Mennonite Church USA, and other charities who do the work that I am unable to do. Although my knowledge is still incomplete, Jesus is why I, a white woman, make an effort to better understand Black and indigenous history.

Recently, my small Mennonite Church in Albany, Oregon, partnered with other ecumenical groups in the area to support a local initiative to provide low-income housing in a "tiny home" community. We hope to continue participating in this effort by supporting two more small communities that will provide refuge and safety. This is one way we listen to Jesus' words to provide justice to others—this is who we say Jesus is.

In reflecting on this passage during the Lenten season, I have begun to wonder whether I place barriers upon others who want to know Jesus and his love. How has my church upheld "religious" attitudes, beliefs, or practices that make it difficult for others to participate? Do we become angry at the injustices we observe? Are we willing to use our anger to bring relief to those who are abused or mistreated?

For reflection

1. How do you respond to an image of an angry Jesus?

2. How do you wish to provide justice to others who have been harmed?

3. What do you do with your anger? Is it directed inward, outward, or repressed? How can you respond in more healthy, life-giving ways?

Prayer

Creator God, you know my thoughts, my heart, my actions. Forgive me when I close my eyes and my heart to others' needs. Forgive me when I get tired of doing what I hear you calling me to do. Open my eyes to you and to others. Help me and our churches to willingly stand alongside those who are seeking justice, health, and wholeness. In Jesus' name, amen.

JESUS BEGINS TO GATHER HIS FOLLOWERS

Nelson Martínez Muñoz (Colombia)

JOHN 1:35–51

v. 39, 41 *"Come and see . . . we have found the Messiah."*

I am the sixth of seven siblings, with the three youngest being boys. We were raised by a Christian mother and by a father who respected our faith. Ever since I was a teenager I have felt a great passion to serve God. However, as a newly-married man I heard a clear call from the Lord. When I accepted that call to serve in God's work, I had to resign from my job in a well-known public company. That decision aroused all kinds of comments among my colleagues and acquaintances. The comment that I remember most was that of an atheist friend who, to my great surprise, told me, "Congratulations!" After noting my surprise, he added, "That new job is going to bring you lots of money."

Our country, Colombia, has high rates of poverty and unemployment and a precarious educational system. This means that many people are engaged in occupations that have nothing to do with their skills or knowledge but are focused instead on meeting their material needs. Sadly, this is a reality from which the church does not escape. Many people decide to pursue religious work as a way out of poverty and unemployment. The false doctrine of prosperity has made the situation worse, since some have turned to preaching as a form of material enrichment.

The way Jesus begins to gather followers (John 1:35–51) is inspiring, at least for those who decide to follow him for legitimate reasons. Some followed Jesus because they heard a reference made to him by their leader (vv. 35–36). Others came to Jesus because of the testimony of someone who already knew him (vv. 41–42). There were also those who followed him in response to a direct call from Jesus (v. 43). But in each case, all of these individuals were impacted by the personal encounter with the Messiah (vv. 41, 45)—an encounter that based following Jesus on a personal relationship, beyond any religious conviction or any interest or gain.

In a world where there is so much pressure for the attainment of personal dreams and goals, it is countercultural for the invitation to follow Jesus to be based on who he is, rather than what he offers. It may not be so appealing to simply say like Nathanael, "You are the Son of God." But when a person understands who Jesus is, they may also understand how insignificant personal dreams and earthly gains are. And they may even hear Jesus say, "Greater things than these you will see," albeit with respect to God's glory, not human glory.

Jesus saw and described Nathanael as "a genuine Israelite in whom there is no deceit" (v. 47). If you were evaluated and described by Jesus as a Christian, what would he say about you?

When I was about to finish my studies at the Biblical Seminary of Colombia (1994), I felt great fear wondering if my ministerial work would be fruitful. Then I heard the voice of Jesus telling me "Remain in me, and I will remain in you. A branch can't produce fruit by itself, but must remain in the vine. Likewise, you can't produce fruit unless you remain in me. I am the vine; you are the branches. If you remain in me and I in you, then you will produce much fruit. Without me, you can't do anything." (John 15:4–5). I understood that the Lord was not demanding fruit from me, but faithfulness.

I understood that fruitfulness as more of a promise than a demand; I only had to occupy myself with remaining in him.

Throughout these thirty years of serving as a pastor among the Mennonite Brethren, my exhortation to the brothers and sisters in the churches I have served has been to walk with Jesus, along with their families. We have sought to engage each person in their personal relationship with God more than their ministry. Numbers, statistics, and goals in ministry have taken a back seat to the priority of a life of wholeness as a result of personal discipleship and following Jesus for who he is.

An old hymn that echoed in my mind that day in 1994 when Jesus spoke to me about abiding in him has since become my life slogan:

Christ, I want to be faithful, give me the power, give me the power.
I want to walk with you without hesitation, without hesitation.
I want to follow in your footsteps, close to you, close to you.
And if I find trials here, grant that I might trust in you.

For Reflection

1. When—or how—have you experienced Jesus calling you to follow him? How has that call changed your life?

2. Jesus saw and described Nathanael as "a genuine Israelite in whom there is no deceit" (v. 47). If you were evaluated and described by Jesus as a Christian, what would he say about you?

Prayer

I pray to God, the sole owner and Savior of the church, to allow the Anabaptist community around the world to continue to be light and salt on earth and to deliver us from the temptations of power-seeking and materialism that have invaded some sectors of the Christian church. I pray that the Lord will protect our global church from cultural influences such as humanism and secularism so that we may serve in such a way as to fulfill the Lord's desire, "that they may see your good works, and glorify your Father in heaven" (Matthew 5:16). Amen.

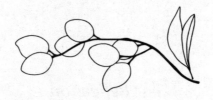

AS JESUS WALKS . . . HE CALLS PETER, ANDREW, JAMES, AND JOHN

Jürg Bräker (Switzerland)

MATTHEW 4:18–22

v. 19 *"Come, follow me," he said, "and I'll show you how to fish for people." Right away, they left their nets and followed him.*

When I was a young teenager, I felt a strong call to become a secondary school teacher. I had experienced my teachers as helpful companions, particularly at a time in life when it seemed like the basic directions for the future were being laid out. It seemed clear that God was calling me to follow in their footsteps.

At about the same time, I was also on a journey toward conversion and baptism. In that process a verse from the book of Haggai touched me deeply. In a context of profound distress, when the temple in Jerusalem was still in ruins and the rebuilding efforts were encountering many obstacles, the prophet Haggai spoke to Zerubbabel, who was about to become Israel's next king: "On that day, says the LORD of heavenly forces: I will take you, Zerubbabel, Shealtiel's son, my servant, says the LORD; I will make you like a signet ring because I have chosen you, says the LORD of heavenly forces" (Haggai 2:23).

This verse awakened something in me—indeed, I have remained attentive to this voice throughout my life. Of course, I was not Zerubbabel, a chosen one in the line of kings of Israel. I was only a young student, not at all sure about where or how my gifts might connect to the broader world. But the phrase "I have chosen you!" touched a deep chord in my being—they were words I was longing to hear.

In the end, my life did not unfold in the linear path I had imagined. The years when I was training to become a teacher were filled with ambiguity. On the one hand, the solid grades I earned in my university classes seemed to confirm that I was on the right path. On the other hand, I was constantly afraid of failing. When I finally entered the teaching profession—after eight years of studies sustained by a strong conviction that this was my calling—I had deep doubts about whether this was where I truly belonged. I also had doubts about my faith. Were there any foundations to what I believed or had I just developed certain habits of faith, adapting to what others believed?

In those years, the promise of "I have chosen you" began to change. Those words had set me on the way, but now I was more like Thomas, the disciple whose doubts compelled him to actually touch the wounds of the crucified Jesus. During that time, I was forced to confront my doubts before God, trusting that God could deal with them. I also sensed a new call—not to believe in my own faith, but to confide in God, trusting that God could sustain me in this period of wavering and uncertainty. When I took some time to examine the sources of my insecurity more carefully, I recognized how much selfish ambition was mixed up with what I had imagined to be my calling.

That time of reflection turned into three years of theological studies in a search for truth, both about myself and about God as the source and the path to all truth.

And then the question of calling reemerged. Should I return to teaching or follow a call to pastoral ministries? I did not hear such a clear voice as I had heard it in my teens. But on a deeper level, I realized that God was calling me into much larger freedom. Christ was walking with me in my choices.

While studying theology in Heidelberg (Germany), a university with many different streams of theology, I realized that my faith was going through a far-reaching transition. As many earlier convictions dissolved, it was not clear what would replace them. During this time, it was Jesus' prayer for his disciples in John 17:24 that held me fast. In that prayer I heard the intimate longing of Christ: "Father, I want those you gave me to be with me where I am." I still hear Jesus praying these words even today. It is his desire that holds me where he is, as I continue to follow that thread of truth-seeking.

In today's devotional passage, Jesus is walking—he is moving. He calls Andrew and then James and John with the invitation: come on the way. What the kingdom would look like changed many times. Yes, Jesus had a vision of the kingdom coming into this world and that the growing community of his disciples would walk toward it together. Yet this journey was not about what they would accomplish or their firm convictions, which often wavered. Instead, the constant refrain of the journey was "I want you to be with me, where I am." Jesus called them to walk with him with hearts open to change in a world of constant change.

When I look back on my journey, I often ask myself: What about that sense of being called in my early teens to walk with people in

54

transition? Today, I realize that that call is still there, despite the fact that I did not continue as a school teacher. In my work as a pastor, I feel most alive when I am doing exactly this—namely, walking with people in transition, often on the margins of their communities. Sometimes it is teenagers, sometimes people who are much older.

To be able to do this, I also had to become someone who could recognize God walking with me in those transitions—as someone who walks between the lines in those spaces of ambiguity where the thirst for truth sometimes means that I need to let go of long-held convictions. Here is where I learn to trust his call: "Come with me on the way. I want you to be where I am." Here is where I learn to trust God's faithfulness—a God who is beyond all my ambiguities and doubts.

For reflection

1. When you look over the journey of your life, what landscapes come to your mind? How did God walk with you in each of those periods in life?

2. What does it mean for you to get up and follow Jesus calling you?

3. Did your experience and knowledge of God change in the course of your life? Where do you see God's faithfulness in your life?

Blessing

As you walk the path of your life,
through pathless forests, full of thorns and trees, teeming with life,
    reaching to the sky,
through wide plains where heaven meets the earth and faraway
    horizons call you,
in deserts, retracing your footsteps in the search for life-giving water,
and up to promising mountain peaks,
may you always know Christ walking alongside you,
walking his way with us toward his kingdom come
in the midst of this world.

JESUS TEACHES THE DISCIPLES HOW TO PRAY

Kari Traoré (Burkina Faso)

MATTHEW 6:5–15

---

vv. 12–13 *"Forgive us for the ways we have wronged you, just as we also forgive those who have wronged us. And don't lead us into temptation, but rescue us from the evil one."*

After praying this familiar prayer once again, I realized that it's impossible to truly enter into Jesus' prayer unless you are a part of him, unless you are a disciple. After all, Jesus is instructing his disciples how to pray. As a disciple of Jesus, I am confident that in my daily life I am nothing without him—I cannot do anything without Jesus in my life. Jesus is my connection to our Father in heaven (v. 9).

Through this connection, I share in the nature and glory of God. Since, by faith, I partake in the image of God, if people love Jesus, they will love me. If they listen to Jesus, they will listen to me. If they insult Jesus, they will insult me too. If they persecute Jesus, they will persecute me too. This is what John says in his gospel:

> The light came to his own people,
>> and his own people didn't welcome him.
> But those who did welcome him,
>> those who believed in his name
> he authorized to become God's children,
>> born not from blood
>> nor from human desire or passion,
>> but born from God.
> The Word became flesh
>> and made his home among us.
> We have seen his glory,
>> glory like that of a father's only son,
>> full of grace and truth. (John 1:11–14)

Addressing God as my Father is a confession that even though I am living on this earth, my ultimate home is not this world but in heaven. At the same time, I pray that God's kingdom and will would be fully revealed on earth—that heaven and earth would be made whole (v. 10).

Jesus is my provider (v. 11). My life depends on him first and not the riches of this earth.

Jesus is also my advocate and my redeemer. As a human I am limited and I continue to sin. This means that I rely every day on his grace and mercy. Though I do my best to pursue justice, I sometimes fail. I need Jesus' daily help in order to be in communion with him. Acknowledging my weakness is a lesson for me as I respond to others. Just as I recognize my own inclination to sin, I know others can sin too, sometimes against me. Just as Jesus forgives me whenever I seek his forgiveness, I too want to be like Jesus in forgiving others for their trespasses (v. 12).

Jesus teaches us to pray "Don't lead us into temptation, but rescue us from the evil one" (v. 13) as a reminder that we cannot overcome the trials and temptations that we face on our own. Moreover, Jesus reminds us that the enemy is not my brother or sister—the only true enemy is the evil one. This prayer reveals that giving our life to Jesus is a declaration of war on the evil one. If we are to be victorious in this battle, we must rely on Jesus alone. He alone is the one who can deliver us and break every bond we have with sin and evil. But just as the evil one was unsuccessful in his battle with Jesus, we also will emerge from the battle victorious because we have been delivered by the triumph of the resurrection of Jesus over the power of the cross.

For reflection

1. If you have memorized the Lord's Prayer, close your eyes and repeat it once again, slowly, in your mind. What stands out to you?

2. What does it mean for you to be "rescued from the evil one"?

3. What are the various ways that you pray? Which are the most comfortable? Which forms of prayer would you like to develop further?

Prayer

Lord, let us reflect your glory as we are bound to you as our heavenly Father. Oh Lord, give us the strength and understanding to forgive our brothers and sisters and even our enemies. Help us recognize that our enemy is not them but the evil one. Oh, Jesus, help us rely on you for our deliverance. We can't win without you. May our light shine before others, that they may see our good deeds and glorify our heavenly Father (Matthew 5:16). Amen.

Part 3

THE KINGDOM
TAUGHT

THE ROCK

Peter Confesses Jesus Is the Christ

Reinhard Kummer (Austria)

MATTHEW 16:13–20

---

v. 15 *"What about you? Who do you say that I am?"*
Simon Peter said, "You are the Christ, the Son of the
living God."

As I was growing up, Austria was still a deeply Roman Catholic country—nearly 90 percent of the population was Catholic. Indeed, my mother had been a novice in a nunnery. Fortunately for me, she left the order before taking her vows of poverty, chastity, and obedience! Even though my parents were not strictly observant Catholics, they were God-fearing in clear and simple ways. Since religious instruction is compulsory in Austrian public schools, Catholics and other faith traditions are required to provide doctrinal teaching in the curriculum. This meant that Catholicism was simply a given for me throughout my childhood. Looking back, I'm deeply grateful to my parents and religion teachers for the fact that I never doubted the existence of God or the truth of the Bible as the Word of God.

In 1976, when I was just twenty-one years old and recently married, Jesus Christ seized me and I encountered him in a real way. That relationship has been part of my life ever since. In the years that followed, many questions emerged that demanded a lot of attention in my new life with Jesus Christ. Although the instruction I had received in school regarding God, Jesus, and the Bible was very rudimentary, it was clear to me from the moment I first encountered Jesus that he was the Messiah, the Son of God, my Savior and Redeemer. To be sure, that conviction corresponded with the teaching of the Catholic Church. But what I had superficially learned about the person of Jesus Christ now became a firm certainty, albeit one that I did not fully understand and could hardly justify. It was simply a force that completely changed me. From that point on, my friends had to endure my enthusiasm about Jesus Christ. Some declared me crazy; others said that this religious phase would pass. Like Peter, I certainly did not have a full understanding at that time about the gospel. Nevertheless, like Peter, I could wholeheartedly affirm that Jesus was indeed the Christ, the Son of the living God.

In our text, Jesus temporarily forbade Peter and the disciples to speak openly about his identity as the Messiah (Matthew 16:20). I, by contrast, took every opportunity possible to talk about Jesus. Along the way, I started to encounter Christians outside the Catholic Church. For example, I became acquainted with a congregation in Vienna that started as a home Bible study group led by Irene and Abe Neufeld, a Mennonite couple from Canada. My wife Rosemarie and I began to attend this congregation regularly. As our relationship with the church grew deeper, the question emerged as to whether we should join the congregation by seeking a baptism of faith in obedience to Jesus Christ's words.

For a long time, however, the words of Jesus to Peter in Matthew 16:18–19 created a profound conflict of conscience. Our infant baptism and our membership in the Roman Catholic church raised deep questions. Catholic doctrine clearly teaches the primacy of the pope and asserts that there is no salvation outside the Catholic Church. These teachings seemed to be justified by Jesus' words to Peter in Matthew 16 and elsewhere in Scripture. Was it possible to leave this church without disobeying God? Should we join a church that did not submit to the authority of the pope, even though Jesus clearly said that he would build his church on Peter, the rock? Could salvation be found outside this church? Is voluntary baptism by faith a true baptism or is only the Roman Catholic sacrament of baptism valid?

For two years, we struggled with these questions of obedience. How could we develop spiritually if, on the one hand, we could not belong to our new spiritual home, the Anabaptist church, where we were being nurtured and where we had been invited to share our gifts? On the other hand, what would it mean to end our connections to the church into which we were received through infant baptism, albeit without our awareness? If we left the Catholic Church, were we leaving the rock on which Jesus Christ built his church? What was the meaning of "binding and loosing"? Would we be lost outside the Catholic Church?

Two thoughts liberated us from our troubled conscience.

First, Jesus speaks of the trust that Peter expressed with his confession that Jesus was the Messiah. The basis of Jesus' church is trust in Jesus Christ. Second, Peter can also refer to a rock that is built on that foundation. As Paul writes to the Corinthians: "No one can lay any other foundation besides the one that is already laid, which is Jesus Christ" (1 Corinthians 3:11).

Even if some theologians have justified a third interpretation—namely, that Peter himself is the rock on which Jesus builds his church—we have found this reading of the text spiritually oppressive and narrow. The first two emphases, by contrast, have broadened our horizons and freed our consciences from bondage and fears.

For this we give thanks to God.

For reflection

1. Are there any constraints in your tradition that might hinder people in their spiritual development?

2. What is the foundation of your church? How do you describe it to those outside your tradition?

3. If you know of other interpretations of Matthew 16:18, I would love to hear from you (reinhard.kummer@mennoniten.at).

Prayer

Thank you, faithful Lord, for your good guidance through your Word and your Holy Spirit. Thank you for your deliverance from narrowness and false bondage. Thank you for comforting our troubled and doubting consciences. Thank you for waiting patiently for our sometimes sluggish and cumbersome understanding. Thank you for your manifold blessings when we have sought your good guidance. Thank you for your promise to be with us until the end of time.

Please free all who are bound in conscience through your Holy Spirit and your Word. Help your church to recognize and loosen its bonds, and to free those who are bound within and outside our communities. Bless your children with the freedom of your glory. Amen.

JESUS ENCOUNTERS THE WOMAN AT THE WELL . . . AND JESUS ENCOUNTERS ME

Cindy Alpízar (Costa Rica)

JOHN 4:4–30

---

v. 13 *"Everyone who drinks this water will be thirsty again, but whoever drinks from the water that I will give will never be thirsty again. The water that I give will become in those who drink it a spring of water that bubbles up into eternal life."*

During those times in life when we feel most empty, we often choose to withdraw from others, not knowing how to deal with the deep pain and trauma that we are carrying. And then, at some surprising moment, Jesus appears, sitting attentively beside the deep wells in which we are submerged, offering compassion, love, encouragement, and a good conversation. It's only after we come to know him, walking together in the journey, that we realize he was always there—supporting and strengthening us, waiting for that special circumstance to make himself visible and chat with us.

So it was for me. In the tender years of my life I felt a deep need to hide my sadness and burdens by trying to make myself useful or by disappearing into my studies where I could find a sense of fulfillment when nothing else in my life was giving me purpose. I grew up in the context of a failed marriage, the daughter of an alcoholic father and a mother whose multiple depressions left her feeling as if she was among the living dead. I survived in my great-grandmother's house, trying to get ahead in a complicated world in the face of many limitations. That was my life in the 1980s in Costa Rica—a country of simple workers where single mothers had few opportunities and a sense of helplessness often felt overwhelming.

Despite carrying this pain along with many doubts for several years, I always sensed that something stronger was out there. It was not very clear; I was still walking in darkness. But there was a voice, a call, a captivating presence that ultimately led me to take action—to take my burden in hand and seek some answers. I did not find philosophies or ideologies in my search. But I was led to a relationship that would change my life forever. The Master did not hide from me, nor did he tell me to be quiet, like others did. Instead, he presented himself as he is, and he assured me that I could set down my pitcher that was overflowing, though not with the water of life.

At one point in the gospels, Jesus invited his disciples to leave their nets and follow him. Now, he asked me to leave behind my burdens— my pitcher filled with worries. His words provided light to illuminate my way. He became my anchor in the storm, my security in the midst of doubt. In him I found purpose, meaning, and my new path.

When I reflect on this passage from John 4, I see that Jesus is willing to challenge traditional assumptions, to ignore barriers faced by women—not just women in general, but this specific woman. She had been living in the shadows, but Jesus singles her out. He sees her as she is and offers himself without hesitation.

In that beautiful conversation, unlike any other recorded in Scripture, Jesus speaks with ease and confidence, offering her not what she had asked for but what she urgently needed—namely, the purpose for which she had been created. "If you recognized God's gift and who is saying to you, 'Give me some water to drink,' you would be asking him and he would give you living water" (John 4:10). He offers her the fullness of life that is a gift of God. He offers himself—simply and transparently. The woman recognizes what he is giving and the truth gushes forth like living water. It floods her heart and fills her with resolve to continue on the way. The woman at the well is restored, transformed, truly seen. And when that happens, one cannot help but share it with others. So she runs to her people, to the same ones that despised her. But now she is empowered by God's love to speak, to show herself as a recipient of transcendent grace that convinced the others.

That same grace came to me. My faith continues to be strengthened as I follow him. I have also understood that the gift given to me must be shared with my friends, acquaintances, and others in my community of faith. What the Lord has given us is a wonderful gift because it grows when it is shared. That is a truth that has been revealed to me, challenging the limitations that we put on ourselves as women in Latin American contexts.

Long ago I left my pitcher and, filled with living water, I have been telling others what has happened to me in the hope that many will return to the road and follow him as well.

For reflection

1. What is the void in your life? What are you still carrying on your journey that has no solution and only fills you with pain?

2. Who do you need Jesus to be for you today—a doctor? a teacher? a father? a husband? a son?

3. Can you let go of your past today and seek a new path forward accompanied by Jesus? Know that Jesus is waiting for you at your well!

Prayer

Today, I ask God for a special blessing for the person who is reading this. I hope that you can be affirmed in your path today; that you can speak clearly about your needs and bring it to the source of living water that is Jesus. By opening your heart, may you be healed of your past pain. May you find new meaning in life and be freed to share with others the living water that he offers you. I pray that that water will not only satisfy your thirst, but will flow out like a gushing river filling everything around you. I call out to Jesus that you might today return to the path that you have perhaps left because of life's problems. May you know the affirmation of our good Master and be confirmed by the clarity of your purpose, so that you may also be an answer for those you encounter who are overwhelmed. The fields are ripe unto harvest, Lord. Send us!

JESUS TEACHES THE PARABLE OF THE RICH FOOL

Gracia Felo (Democratic Republic of the Congo)

LUKE 12:13–21

---

v. 15 *Then Jesus said to them, "Watch out! Guard yourself against all kinds of greed. After all, one's life isn't determined by one's possessions, even when someone is very wealthy."*

In this parable Jesus challenges his listeners to sort out what is truly important in life. Someone in the crowd thinks he has not received his fair share of an inheritance. Jesus responds by telling a story that reframes the question entirely. We all are going to die! What are we doing now to prepare ourselves for the things that really matter? How can we learn to be "rich toward God" (Luke 12:21)?

One evening several years ago I was in the local parish compound for an evening service when I spotted a group of three young teenagers smoking marijuana. I was curious, but also troubled. When I approached them for a conversation, they didn't move. But I noticed that one young man was hiding his marijuana. The others continued to smoke calmly in my presence. Although I didn't know them well, they all lived in my neighborhood. So I greeted them. "You're so young," I said, "not even fifteen. It's not good for you. Smoking marijuana has a lot of health consequences." We talked for about ten minutes as I encouraged them to stop smoking. Then we parted company.

A few days later, I again bumped into Manasseh, the young man who had hidden his marijuana. During our brief conversation, I asked him if he prayed. When he responded no, I took the opportunity to invite him to our Sunday church service. He assured me that he would attend, but after several weeks I noticed that he had still not come to our prayer services. When I encountered him again a few weeks later and asked why he hadn't attended the service, I was surprised by his answer: "I don't have the right clothes to come to Sunday worship service." I promised to find a solution.

It didn't take long for me to find some comfortable clothes in his size in my closet, along with a pair of shoes. When I arrived at his home, his mother informed me that Manasseh was out with his friends. But when she heard the reason for my visit, she was delighted since she was also a Christian. She encouraged me to persevere. So I asked her to give the parcel to Manasseh.

The following Sunday, Manasseh came to church service, where he was welcomed with great enthusiasm and kindness by all the church members. Sometime later, I persuaded him to resume his high school studies, which he had stopped several years prior. Along the way, he continued to participate regularly in various church and youth department services.

Thanks to the love of the Lord and the love of the church, Manasseh gradually began to give up drugs. He learned to pray, to meditate on the Bible, and to develop relationships with other church members.

Today, Manasseh lives with his family in the capital city of Kinshasa (DRC) where, little by little, he continues to grow in his Christian life.

Jesus has an infinite love for lost souls. He cares deeply about those who have lost their way, and he uses us to share with the world the infinite riches with which he has endowed us.

As Jesus tells us in Luke 12:13–21, forsaking evil and accepting the kingdom of God as Manasseh did is a greater form of wealth and wisdom. Many people are immersed in their occupations, in entertainment, drink, drugs, money, sex, or other worldly pleasures, thinking they are rich. However, the Bible teaches us that all this is foolish. It is foolish to be rich for oneself, but great wisdom to be rich for God. We become rich in God when we abandon evil and submit ourselves to God's will.

For reflection

1. What words, phrases, or images stand out for you as you read and reflect on this parable?

2. The story begins with someone who appeals to Jesus' sense of justice in the hopes of receiving a fair portion of his inheritance. How do you think this person felt when he heard Jesus' response?

3. Many Christians have argued that wealth—especially wealth earned through wise investments—is a clear sign of Christian maturity and God's favor. Is this teaching to be taken seriously?

Prayer

Lord Jesus, thank you for the riches found in you and your heavenly kingdom. Give us the strength and wisdom not just to hoard riches for ourselves, but rather to be rich for you.

JESUS AND ZACCHAEUS: AN ENCOUNTER OF TRANSFORMING LOVE

Willi Hugo Pérez (Guatamala)

LUKE 19:1–10

vv. 9–10 *Jesus said to him, "Today, salvation has come to this household because he too is a son of Abraham. The Human One came to seek and save the lost."*

The good news—or gospel—is about transforming love. The good news is a saving grace that welcomes, includes, heals, and restores. It is a grace that gives new life, producing in those who receive it the fruits of repentance, reconciliation, peace, mercy, and solidarity in our relationships with those around us. It is a love that leads us into encounters with others—those who are needy, vulnerable, marginalized, strangers, or enemies—so that we can embrace and bless them. Such a redemptive power is portrayed beautifully in the story of Jesus' encounter with Zacchaeus as narrated in the gospel of Luke.

Luke invites us to meet Zacchaeus, a Jewish tax collector for the Romans, who has become rich by exploiting others. Because of this activity, Zacchaeus has a bad reputation among his countrymen. They regard him as impure—as a sinner with whom all associations should be avoided.

But human failings and weaknesses do not reveal everything that is in a person's heart. Perhaps out of curiosity—or, more likely, because deep down he is looking for something more in life—Zacchaeus wants to meet Jesus. So when Jesus passes through Jericho, Zacchaeus runs to meet him.

Zacchaeus, however, is short of stature. He has a hard time seeing Jesus in the crowd. So he climbs a tree to get a better view. And there the unimaginable happens. Jesus sees Zacchaeus. Their eyes meet. Jesus regards him with love and mercy, and tells him that he wants to stay in Zacchaeus's home. Filled with joy, Zacchaeus comes down from the tree and prepares to receive Jesus into his house. Later, he will also take Jesus into his heart.

As the story continues, Jesus, who refuses to judge according to appearances, ignores the murmurings of those who reproach him for associating with an impure, public sinner and enters Zacchaeus's house. Then, moved by this welcoming attitude and the merciful, comforting words of Jesus, Zacchaeus opens his heart.

His conversion translates into a new way of life, including concrete acts of love and generosity towards his neighbors. As a tangible expression of his repentance, Zacchaeus makes a conscious decision to redirect the course of his life. He decides to share his possessions generously with the poor, giving away half of his possessions, and compensating those he had defrauded four times over. "Today, salvation has come to this household," Jesus says, pleased, "because he too is a son of Abraham."

How marvelous! Jesus—who neither marginalizes nor excludes, the one who has come "to seek and to save that which was lost"—redeems Zacchaeus and restores him to life. Zacchaeus will no longer be the same. He has found a new and abundant life; he has found the true meaning of life.

Like Zacchaeus, I have had a transforming encounter with Jesus. As a ten-year-old boy, I suffered the tragic loss of my father. He was kidnapped and killed during the time of the armed conflict in my country. My family was shattered with pain, sadness, and grief. Several other innocent families in my village, and thousands of people in my country, suffered from that cruel war. Damaged by that violent trauma, traumatized by that violence, I became bitter, selfish, and hardened by pain. How could I have imagined that Jesus would come to regard me with love and restore my life? But he did. In my early twenties, I was lost in a dark tunnel of resentment, alcoholism, violence, and bitterness. In my desperation I sought Jesus. From my heart I cried out, "Jesus, if you really exist and remember me, maybe you would want to help me." And Jesus looked at me with tenderness and compassion. His merciful grace dissipated the mists that enveloped my life and brought healing for my hatred and pain. Since then, he has led me on a path of liberation, restoration, and healing. I have found hope and new life. And having received his forgiveness, I was able to forgive those who had hurt me so much.

To encounter Jesus is to find the true meaning of life. Jesus redeems us, heals us, restores us, and gives us peace. Moreover, his restoring love leads us to encounter the other—the needy, the marginalized, the stranger, and the enemy, the one we have hurt, the one who has hurt us. In those encounters, we discover that person's humanity and recognize them as a brother or sister. With humility, joy, and gratitude I can say, "Lord Jesus, you are my savior, my healer, and my teacher. You are my light and my peace!"

In Jesus we see God's sublime grace and God's healing mercy. Jesus, who has compassion for all, knows how to see beyond the weaknesses, sins, failures, and miseries that tarnish our dignity. He restores our humanity. He wants to heal and save everyone; he invites everyone to follow him.

If we allow him to dwell in us, he redeems and blesses us, restoring us to our true condition as sons and daughters of God. He makes us a new creation so that we may do the good and generous works that he desires. He invites us to live in the kingdom of God—to share in this community of love, life, justice, reconciliation, communion, and peace.

In our Central American countries—so beautiful and promising, yet at the same time damaged by so much sin, evil, violence, injustice, and exclusion—Jesus continues to seek us out, calling us to follow him. Like Zacchaeus, those who encounter his transforming love and receive it in their hearts become themselves expressions of love, mercy, justice, life, and joy, forerunners of a new, reconciled, and peaceful world.

For reflection

1. How do we best describe the way salvation comes into our life, our homes, and our communities?

2. Are we capable of truly looking at people—understanding their reality and walking beside them with empathy and tender acceptance—as Jesus did?

3. Jesus went to meet Zacchaeus with an attitude of genuine mercy and welcome. This opened Zacchaeus's heart and set him on the path of transformation. What is our attitude when we encounter others—our neighbors or those who need us? How do we look upon the vulnerable, the despised and the excluded? How do we welcome them?

4. As people of faith and a community of Jesus, what changes are we helping to bring about in our community or context? What signs of hope do we see?

Prayer

Beloved Jesus, you are able to see beyond our failings and weaknesses. Like Zacchaeus, we want to know you better, but so many things prevent us from doing so. Look upon us and restore us with your tender mercy. Let your salvation come into our lives and our land. Restore to us the dignity of being sons and daughters of God. Enkindle in us the fire of love for our neighbors. Give us just, generous, and merciful hearts capable of welcoming the marginalized, the needy, the betrayed, the enemies, and those who suffer without hope. Help us to testify and proclaim with joy that you are the Christ, the Son of the Living God, our Lord and Savior!

JESUS TEACHES ABOUT SERVICE AND GIVES WARNINGS

Valentina Kunze (Uruguay)

MARK 9:33–50

v. 37 *"Whoever welcomes one of these children in my name welcomes me; and whoever welcomes me isn't actually welcoming me but rather the one who sent me."*

At the beginning of this passage Jesus responds to a question that the disciples had been debating among themselves: Which of them was the greatest? Who was the most worthy? Who was the best follower of Jesus? Even though they didn't ask Jesus to resolve their debate, he knew what they were talking about and he openly addressed the issue. He called the disciples together, sat down with them, and told them bluntly: "Whoever wants to be first must be least of all and the servant of all" (v. 35). Then he reinforced his teaching by offering an object lesson: he embraced a child, and identified himself—and God!—with the status of children.

All this sounds so contrary to our experience and what society has taught us. What, exactly, does Jesus mean by this? How does this work?

Clearly, the topic is important to him. Even after John changes the subject (v. 38), Jesus comes back to the same theme. He takes the time to explain it to the disciples because he wants to be sure that they understand what he meant—how we treat the people Jesus loves matters! Even small acts of kindness offered to someone Jesus loves brings great rewards (vv. 37, 41). By the same token, causing someone that he loves to fall—including ourselves (see vv. 43–48)—carries huge adverse consequences (v. 42).

What I see in this text is that Jesus loves people . . . a lot! He loves each person. He's passionate about us. And the implications are clear. If we want to be important in God's kingdom, we also need to love people as much as he does—by putting them first and by rejecting sin, which brings so much harm.

For several years I've been serving in my church in Ciudad de la Costa (Iglesia Menonita de la Costa), as a youth leader. Our small group of teenagers consists of about fifteen kids who come from very different backgrounds. This diversity sometimes makes it challenging to bring the group together. For example, one girl from the group had a particularly hard time integrating with the others. She didn't come from a church background and only joined the group because a school friend had invited her to come along. She didn't know much about Jesus. One week I had set up a one-on-one meeting with her to deepen our relationship—to share the gospel and help her come closer to our church community.

But on the morning when we were scheduled to meet I started having a lot of doubts. What if I couldn't handle the difficulties I would face in light of her background? What if this led to her getting too dependent on me instead of Jesus? What if this meeting wasn't God's will for me? Many more negative thoughts started to invade my mind. I was working from home and had to stop for a moment because I suddenly felt completely overwhelmed. I went to my bed and started praying: "Jesus, I can't do this. I need to call this off. I can't even deal with my thoughts about it."

In that moment Jesus showed me that my responsibilities were actually much simpler than I thought. Love is not that complicated. In the end, all I had to do was to love her; he would do all the rest.

We met that afternoon and ended up having an awesome time together. All my worries and self-doubt had been in vain. I had forgotten to see her as Jesus sees her.

This doesn't mean that every part of the relationship is going to be easy in the future. But Jesus loves her and I want to be on that same side, serving and loving her. This simple, ordinary experience reminded me that Jesus is actually interested in these small details— both the individuals we encounter and our own worries and fears.

I want to challenge you to do your best to see people the way Jesus sees them. To value them as he does. To treat them as gently as you would embrace a child.

For reflection

1. How do you balance appropriate self-care with the radical self-denial that Jesus holds up to his disciples as the "cost of discipleship"?

2. Search yourself openly and honestly. Are any of your actions causing someone else to fall into sin?

3. What acts of service, no matter how small, can you give someone today?

Prayer

Jesus, we're sorry that so often we fail to see others the way you do—as so valuable that you gave your life for them. Forgive us for not recognizing that the time and resources that you entrusted to us are meant to be shared with others. Lord, we apologize for the moments where we put our own needs first and, in so doing, have caused harm to others. Help us to see the needs of those around us, and to respond wisely and with joy. Finally, remove from our lives any habits that cause us to sin. Lord, open our vision towards what you want us to see.

Part 4

THE KINGDOM
LIVED

THE TOUCH OF SHALOM

Cynthia Peacock (India)

MARK 8:22–26

---

v. 25 *Then Jesus placed his hands on the man's eyes again. He looked with his eyes wide open, his sight was restored, and he could see everything clearly.*

Who is Jesus to me? How have I—an Indian woman living in Kolkata with deep connections to Mennonite Central Committee (MCC) and Mennonite World Conference—experienced Jesus?

India is a densely populated country where many live in remote villages with little opportunity to access the services to which they are entitled and which could help meet their basic needs. For more than eighty years, MCC has been working in India, making a positive difference for many of its people, regardless of caste or creed.

Throughout much of my time as an employee of MCC, Mother Teresa, well-known for her work with the very poor in Kolkata, lived close to our office. Every morning people from distant villages and the slums of Kolkata came to line up at Mother Teresa's gate for a handout of food. I often witnessed the deep reverence with which they greeted her by bending down and touching her feet. I saw joy on their faces as they left the queue, holding the food she had given them.

I admired Mother Teresa. But I also knew that many criticized her for the dependency these daily handouts seemed to foster. As someone who basically agreed with MCC's emphasis on interdependency and cooperation, I often wondered whether her daily handouts were making people too dependent on the status quo.

One day, however, I started to see things differently. That morning Mother Teresa, who often visited us while collecting food items, used clothing, and health kits for her institutions, joined our staff to lead our daily devotions. After she had finished sharing her thoughts about how we are called to be God's co-workers in helping to alleviate hunger, a foreign guest whom we were hosting asked the question we all had been wanting to raise: had she ever thought about how her daily food distribution might make people become dependent on her instead of becoming self-dependent by working for their food?

Mother Teresa's response was soft but clear. "MCC and the Mennonites are great friends of mine, and they are doing admirable work to bring dignity to people's lives by not giving them fish to eat, but by teaching them to fish. That is your calling, and I respect that. But my calling is to feed the hungry, clothe the naked, and visit the sick. I do this in obedience to Jesus, and I see him every day in every person I meet, knowing that he or she is in some kind of need."

We were speechless. Her direct and simple response opened my eyes to a new understanding of how Mother Teresa conscientiously imitated Jesus, and why people around the world continue to support her work even today.

I see many parallels between Mother Teresa's life and the teachings embedded in this story from the gospel of Mark. Why, we might ask, did Jesus touch the blind man *twice* to complete his healing? After reflecting further on this text, I am convinced that Jesus touched the man twice to both confirm the man's faith and to invite him to touch Jesus back! By touching the man twice, Jesus healed him both physically and spiritually. Similarly, Mother Teresa served the poor by addressing their physical needs without question, while also tending to their relational and spiritual needs.

I have often needed that same kind of complete healing. I have experienced many stormy times that have tried my soul. But in the process of falling and then being lifted up by God's faithfulness, I would come to realize that the "storm" was behind me. Why? Because every day, even in the worst circumstances of those dark times, I have also felt Jesus' touch, his healing presence.

Like Mother Teresa, I want to take Jesus' teachings more literally and to more conscientiously imitate him in my daily life. Like the blind man, we can know Jesus and be touched by him again and again. Our sight can be restored!

For reflection

1. What is it about human touch that makes it such a powerful message of care and love?

2. How can we know when it's appropriate to give someone a fish, and when it's time to teach that person how to fish?

3. When we help or give something to a friend or stranger in need, a gift of joy is exchanged between the giver and the recipient. When have you experienced this gift as a giver? When have you experienced this as a recipient?

Prayer

Our loving Creator God, thank you that your Spirit lives in us to fulfill your purpose. Help us to be "salt" and "light" to those living in hopelessness. May we point them to Jesus, our Healer and Redeemer. Amen!

JESUS HEALS A DEMON-POSSESSED MAN

Desalegn Abebe (Ethiopia)

LUKE 8:26–39

v. 35 *People came to see what had happened. They came to Jesus and found the man from whom the demons had gone. He was sitting at Jesus' feet, fully dressed and completely sane. They were filled with awe.*

When I was a child growing up in Ethiopia many people followed traditional folkways, which included a deep fear of demons. They consulted witches to get rid of evil spirits. They gave cattle, money, and other resources to witch doctors to protect themselves from evil. People often obeyed orders given to them by the witches. My parents also grew up in this kind of life.

About fifty years ago, when the gospel was preached in my community of Amuru for the first time, people began to say, "Jesus is the

God who frees people from demons." Two Christians who came to teach at a public school prayed for a woman who had been sick for many years because of demonic oppression. Through their prayers, the woman was freed from the demonic bondage. When the teachers rebuked the evil spirits in the name of Jesus, the demons screamed and left her. Then she arose and ate. People had carried her to the home of the teachers; but when she was healed she walked back to her home.

People who heard about this miracle quickly began to spread the word that "Jesus appeared in Amuru." Then people from the district and neighboring districts also came to hear the gospel. Many believed in Christ and were freed from the bondage of demons. This was the starting point for the formation of the Meserete Kristos Church in western Ethiopia.

Ever since I came to faith in the Lord Jesus Christ, I have believed in the supremacy of Christ's authority, and I pray every day for his protection. I believe that through prayer I can overcome the daily challenges I face in Jesus' name, including those caused by demonic influence.

I am now the president of the Meserete Kristos Church, a position of great responsibility. Every day I face new challenges in my life. I rely on Christ's presence to do God's will in these decisions. We know that Satan often tempts those in leadership. Sometimes the temptations come from people with evil intentions. I have learned that I need to love such people, but I also need to identify and defeat their evil agenda in the name of Jesus.

Evil spirits often keep people from living the life God has intended for them. Their purpose is to torture people, separating them from good social relations and making their lives miserable. Humans cannot free others from demonic oppression, but Jesus does have this authority. Jesus is a liberator! Jesus came to this earth so that people can be freed from demonic oppression and experience life in abundance.

As I preach the gospel I pray for people so that they can be freed from the shackles of demons. I have been used by the Holy Spirit to cast out demons from many people through prayer. I know that the name of Jesus is above the power of demons—his name shakes demons, commands them, and casts them out of people.

Jesus set me and other people free from demonic oppression not just to live comfortably but to tell others about all the good things he has done for us so that people can come to him and gain eternal life. When I share the gospel with people and quote a verse from the Bible, they often argue with me. But when I talk about the wonderful changes he has made in my life they are amazed. A testimony to a transformed life has more power to influence others to believe in the gospel than words alone.

The demon-possessed man in this story from the gospel of Luke was helpless. Jesus healed him as an act of grace. Throughout his ministry, Jesus cared for people. I also have experienced God's grace in my life and ministry. I have nothing to be proud of that was achieved on my own—I simply want to follow his example.

The health Jesus offered was holistic. In our church, we often focus on spiritual healing. We strive for people to believe in Christ and to receive the promise of eternal life. In the past, we have given less attention to people's health, economy, education, and social life. Recently, however, we have come to recognize the importance of holistic service. We still have a lot to learn from other churches in this regard.

For reflection

1. How much do you believe in Jesus' authority over evil spirits? How do you practice this in your daily life?

2. What do you learn from the healed person's response in the story from Luke? How ready are you to share what Jesus has done for you with other people?

3. Beyond offering words of encouragement, how do you show care for people who are suffering?

4. What is the holistic transformation that Jesus has brought about in your life?

Prayer

God, our Father, we thank you for freeing us from evil powers. We pray that your authority over demons will set many free from various types of bondage today. May your Spirit enable us to share the good things you have done for us with others. Thank you for hearing our prayers. In the name of Jesus, amen!

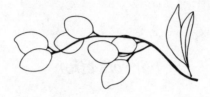

JESUS TEACHES THE PARABLE OF THE GOOD SAMARITAN

Preshit Rao (India)

LUKE 10:25–37

v. 29 *"And who is my neighbor?"*

The parable of the good Samaritan is a favorite story of nearly all ages. And for good reason. Jesus told the parable as a response to two of the most significant questions that a person can ask.

The first question, brought to Jesus as a kind of test by an expert in the law, was: "What must I do to gain eternal life?" (v. 25). Jesus asked him what the law had to say. And so the man answered, "You must love the Lord your God with all your heart, with all your being, with all your strength, and with all your mind, and love your neighbor as yourself." Jesus responded by simply affirming his answer: "Do this and you will live" (v. 28).

But the man, still hoping to trap Jesus, asked a second question: "Who is my neighbor?" (v. 29). Here, instead of answering directly, Jesus tells the parable of "the good Samaritan."

We have been enacting this parable in my church in Rajnandgaon since we were young children in Sunday school. The story imparts a powerful lesson. As kids, the story taught us about sacrificial giving, love, kindness, and compassion. It confirms the message that Jesus is *Jehovah Jireh*, our Provider and Sustainer. Even when times are difficult and we feel like the person beaten by robbers and left to die, God will provide for all our needs in his perfect time through his perfect plan. As we read in Philippians 4:19, "And my God will meet all your needs according to the riches of his glory in Christ Jesus" (NIV).

The Lord has been good and gracious to me throughout my life, continually demonstrating that he has a plan for my life. As a child, I was blessed with a beautiful family who made sure that I was taught the lessons from the Bible. I have been blessed with a good fellowship in my church. God wonderfully supported me during my time in high school and college, when I experienced God's guidance every day. By the grace of God, I received a good education which has now enabled me to serve God and his people through my profession. God has been faithful in answering my prayers. He has been my Provider and Sustainer all my life.

Our country has also been blessed with Christian missionaries from all over the world who left their comfortable lives and luxurious homes to come to our country and to serve among those who were less privileged. They helped to provide us with a good education system and healthcare services. And they also brought the message of good news so that we came to accept Jesus and to follow in his way. We are indeed grateful.

And so as people who have been richly blessed by God, we, as a family, do our best to allow God to use us in service to others. Like the good Samaritan we desire to be a blessing and a helping hand to members of our church and the people around us who are vulnerable or in need. We look for opportunities to show love, kindness, and compassion to others, which is only possible through Christ Jesus.

One example occurred several years ago during the COVID-19 pandemic. People all around the world were going through very difficult times. Although we also were affected, God nevertheless enabled us to become helping hands to needy people around us. Nearly all the members of our church, regardless of their profession, came forward to help our community in every possible way. Some distributed basic necessities like rice, flour, sugar, or oil. Some distributed masks, sanitizers, and oxygen cylinders. In many different ways, the pandemic challenged us to embody the work of the good Samaritan.

More recently, some of the believers in our region were persecuted by their families and villagers for their new faith. They had to flee from their homes and villages to save their lives. In response, the members of our church started a campaign to provide for the needs of our brothers and sisters. We ensured that they had a place for shelter outside the village. People donated clothes, blankets, groceries, and other necessities. All these things were collected in the church and then transported to the refugee camps. It was wonderful to see our believers responding with such generous hearts.

I praise God for this beautiful parable given in the Bible that inspires us to stand out from the crowd and to share God's love with others.

For reflection

1. When have you felt like the unfortunate traveler, beaten down and abandoned alongside the road?

2. Who has been a loving neighbor—or a good Samaritan—to you?

3. What sacrifices or risks are you willing to take to be a good Samaritan to others?

Prayer

Our heavenly Father! Open our eyes to the needs of others and enable us to become channels of blessings to those around us. Give us kind and caring hearts; make us eager to share your love with others. Lord, bless those families who have sacrificially served and cared for the needy. Bless the hands of their labor and may they lack no good thing. In the precious name of Jesus, we pray. Amen.

JESUS FORGIVES A WOMAN ACCUSED OF ADULTERY

Barbara Hege-Galle (Germany)

JOHN 8:1–11

vv. 11 *"Neither do I condemn you. Go, and from now on, don't sin anymore."*

Today is Good Friday, the day in which we remember the death of Jesus. I grew up in a Mennonite family on a small farm in Germany. From childhood, I learned that Jesus is the Savior and Redeemer of the world. As a teenager, our congregation did not have a youth group, so I attended the group of a neighboring Protestant church. In the time leading up to Easter, we always took time to reflect deeply on the meaning of Jesus' death for us. I remember an afternoon of silence when we were asked to focus intensively on our sins—especially on how much Jesus sacrificed for us and how he took our sins upon himself. I returned home very depressed. Was I really such a bad person? Did God's grace for me really depend entirely on such a sacrifice?

I don't think so. I have come to know God as merciful and gracious, full of love and concern for us as humans. This is why God came into the world as Jesus; this is why God became human—not only to suffer and die, but to give us freedom and life.

Since then, I have come to see Jesus as my companion and intercessor. This is also who he was for the woman who was caught in adultery and dragged before the religious leaders. They wanted to punish her. According to the law, she was condemned to death by stoning. Since the men presided as judges over such cases, they could have carried out the punishment directly. Instead, they brought her before Jesus and asked him: "What do you have to say?"

In the end, their primary concern, it seems, was not this woman and her offense. Instead, they wanted to put Jesus to the test. They had often witnessed Jesus placing people above the law and they were looking for reasons to accuse him.

In this situation, however, Jesus did not respond immediately; nor did he respond to their question with a direct answer. Instead, he bent down and wrote in the sand with his finger, giving them time to reflect. Then he challenged them to look deeply within themselves: "Whoever hasn't sinned should throw the first stone." Then he bent down and again wrote in the sand.

I see this woman in front of me, terrified, surrounded by judges. A deep tension lingers in the air. What will happen next? And then, one by one, the men leave. Jesus' answer to their question—"What do you have to say?"—prompted these judgmental religious leaders to leave the confrontation in shame.

Then Jesus straightened up and, seeing the woman standing there alone, he spoke to her: "Woman, where are they? Is there no one to condemn you? . . . Neither do I condemn you!" (v. 10).

A stone must have fallen from the woman's heart—the stone that was supposed to kill her. Jesus not only freed her from her immediate fear of death; he also gave her a new perspective on her life going forward. "Go," he said, "and from now on, don't sin anymore" (v. 11).

If I was to say who Jesus is for me, I would turn to this story. Jesus looks at us with mercy and love. He forgives us. He trusts us to follow him. Our calling is not to judge others, but to respond to injustice clearly and courageously because we ourselves live out of the grace and forgiveness extended to us by Jesus.

In that sense I still confess that Jesus is Savior and Redeemer—he leads us into life.

To summarize, I wholeheartedly affirm the poetic words of the Swiss theologian and poet Kurt Marti:

> Who is Jesus for me? Someone who is at my side.
> How do I think of him? That he tenderly cares for me.
> *[Wer Jesus für mich ist? Einer er für mich ist.*
> *Was ich von ihm halte? Dass er mich hält.]*

For reflection

1. How are the words *redeemer* and *savior* connected with Jesus for you?

2. How might you express who Jesus is without using biblical language? How does this understanding of Jesus impact your life and your ministry?

3. Write a prayer in which you tell Jesus how important he is in your personal life and in the life of the church.

Prayer

Thank you, Jesus, that you see me. You are by my side, my friend and companion. You allow me to work in your kingdom. You give me the strength to remain with you even in difficult circumstances. Thank you, God, for coming into this world; for taking upon yourself a death on the cross so that I might live. Let me become ever more merciful and keep me from judging others. Amen.

JESUS, THE MERCIFUL SAVIOR

Sunoko Lin (Indonesia/United States)

JOHN 5:1–15

---

v. 8–9 *Jesus said to him, "Get up! Pick up your mat and walk." Immediately the man was well, and he picked up his mat and walked.*

Once, at a crucial moment in his ministry, Jesus asked his disciples, "Who do you say that I am?" (Matthew 16:15). The disciples, of course, had accompanied Jesus in his ministry and witnessed his many miracles. But now, based on that personal experience, they faced this critical question. While we do not have the privilege of walking with Jesus in person like the disciples, we do have Scripture that can shape our understanding of Jesus and inform how we should live our lives.

In our text for today we read the story of an encounter between a crippled man and Jesus. This text is deeply meaningful to me because it reveals Jesus' identity as the merciful Savior.

First, Jesus immediately had sympathy for the crippled man and offered to heal him because he knew that the man had suffered for thirty-eight years (v. 6). However, the man did not respond kindly to Jesus' invitation of "Do you want to get well?" (v. 6). Instead, he complained, "I don't have anyone who can put me in the water when it is stirred up" (v. 7). Jesus could have interpreted this response as a "No." But Jesus did not walk away. Instead, he commanded the man to stand up, pick up his mat and walk. And he was healed (vv. 8–9).

Second, Jesus was the merciful Savior because Jesus cared about the man's spiritual and emotional well-being as well as his physical health. After his healing, the Pharisees confronted the man because he violated Jewish law by picking up his mat on the Sabbath (Jeremiah 17:21–22). The Pharisees saw the man through the lens of tradition. By nurturing his faith, Jesus looked at him as someone in need of healing—in both body and soul. After the scolding from the Pharisees, Jesus "found" the man in the temple (v. 14). This is the same word used in other well-known parables of Jesus, as when Jesus finds the lost sheep, the lost coin, or the lost son (Luke 15: 4-6, 8-9, 24, 32). There, Jesus tends to the man's spiritual well-being by exhorting him to live well and to sin no more (John 5:14).

Third, the healing takes place at the pool named Bethesda, which means "mercy." This does not happen by accident. The healing of the crippled man is one of the seven miracles recorded in the gospel of John. Biblical scholars refer to these miracles as signs that help readers understand the identity of Jesus. Both the healing act of Jesus and the place of healing signal to us that Jesus is the merciful Savior.

This is how Jesus found me too. Like the crippled man, I have tasted the mercy of Jesus. I grew up in Indonesia in a Buddhist home. As a teenager, I struggled with suicidal thoughts. I never attended church or Bible study groups. However, one Sunday in September, my high school friend invited me to a student fellowship in my school. That Sunday afternoon, Jesus found me. For the first time I heard the message of life: "I have come that you may have life" (John 10:10). There was no altar call. But returning home, I went to my bedroom and prayed: "If this promise is for me, save me from my dark thoughts." Since that evening, September 22, 1986, I have been set free from the dark thoughts of suicide. I found life because Jesus is the merciful Savior.

Just as Jesus sought the crippled man, we as followers of Jesus must seek the well-being of others. Recently, an older member of our church, Maranatha Christian Fellowship, suffered end-stage renal failure and was put under palliative care in a nursing home. He could no longer attend our Sunday service. Knowing that he missed the church family, we decided to hold a mini–Sunday service when we came to visit on Sunday and brought him his favorite Indonesian dishes. Our visit did not miraculously heal the man, but the nurses told us that our visit was meaningful because it communicated our care, love, and assurance that he was not alone.

When the crippled man complained that there was "no one to help him," Jesus had regard for him, assuring him that he was not alone. There, at Bethesda, the merciful Savior healed him in body and spirit.

If you are feeling crippled and alone, know that the merciful Savior is ready to heal you as well.

For reflection

1. Have you ever felt crippled or paralyzed by a challenge that seems to have been with you for most of your life?

2. In the biblical story, the crippled man initially looks for others to help him into the healing pool. Instead, Jesus invites him to stand up on his own. How, if at all, might this detail be relevant to your circumstances?

3. How have you experienced the merciful Savior in your life?

Prayer

Jesus, merciful Savior, I am deeply grateful that you did not leave me alone. You saved me from despair. When I could not see my purpose, you brought light into my life. Now, I pray that you will give strength to those facing a hard time. Give hope to those facing crises in their lives. Give comfort to those immersed in pain and suffering so that they can endure their present challenge knowing that you are near and ready to help. In the precious name of the merciful Savior, amen.

Part 5

THE UPSIDE-
DOWN KINGDOM

LEADERSHIP IS SERVING RATHER THAN BEING SERVED

Nelson Okanya (Kenya/United States)

LUKE 22:24–30

vv. 25–26 NRSVue *"The kings of the gentiles lord it over them, and those in authority over them are called benefactors. But not so with you; rather, the greatest among you must become like the youngest and the leader like one who serves."*

I was born and raised in Kenya, Africa. In my early childhood and young adulthood in Kenya, it never occurred to me that leadership was in some way associated with servanthood—there were leaders and there were servants. Servants did what leaders told them to do. Put differently, leaders told people what to do, and in many cases commanded unquestionable allegiance and respect. In my recollection, people fought for leadership positions and then made sure they and their relatives benefitted from their power.

The story of Jesus and his disciples in this passage shows a different approach to leadership.

The immediate context of this text is the Jewish Passover. Passover was the Jewish celebration of their liberation from oppression—a time to feel safe, free, and secure. This, however, was not an ordinary Passover. Jesus was to become the lamb that takes away the sin of the world (John 1:29). As he and his disciples traveled to Jerusalem, his sacrificial death for the salvation of the world was imminent. It is therefore surprising to read that "a dispute also arose among them." It is even more baffling to discover that the dispute was about who among them was the greatest (v. 24 NRSVue, here and following). In the larger context of Luke 22 the preceding argument about who would betray Jesus (v. 23) makes sense. But the subsequent argument about greatness leaves the reader with many questions.

In the midst of this debate, Jesus seized on the moment to do some teaching about leadership. The model of leadership the disciples understood best was top-down rule. Jesus called it "lording it over" the people. In the biblical context such leaders were revered and honored as "benefactors" (v. 25). In his commentary on Luke, Fredrick W. Danker explains the meaning of the Greek word, *euergétēs*, as those who "conceal tyranny under extravagant expenditure."[4] Such leaders command allegiance and loyalty by creating the illusion that their followers, communities, or even churches, cannot afford to lose them.

Jesus turns the tables on that model and introduces an alternative model of leadership that defines "greatness" as "serving." Indeed, among his disciples Jesus was the "one who serves" (v. 27). And he promised to continue serving them at his own table where they would sit as judges over the twelve tribes of Israel (v. 30). Jesus, the servant, is the new model for the disciples' understanding of leadership. In the community he has formed, leaders are to serve others, not themselves.

At James Street Mennonite Church, we highly value serving our community and the world. We serve our neighbors through programs led by volunteers as well as through more spontaneous opportunities. In doing so, we seek to align our lives with his life and teachings.

My work takes me to many different countries around the world. One of the attitudes that I have repeatedly encountered in my travels is that leaders often expect to have "your time to eat." In other words, leaders assume that they will go to the front of the line and enjoy easy access to available resources—personal interests are a priority. The servant leader model of Jesus subverts top-down rule, benefactor attitudes, and personal interests.

In his teaching and example, we learn that true leadership is rooted in loving and serving others.

For reflection

1. Do you and people in leadership around you know the qualities and behaviors of true greatness? How do you measure your value or worth as a leader?

2. Is leadership the same as position? If not, what role does position have in leadership?

3. What implications does Jesus' upside-down model of leadership have for you and your community?

Prayer

Lord Jesus, open our eyes to see what you see and our ears to hear what you hear and what you say. Move our feet to bring good news to your creation and our hands to gently hold the vulnerable among us. Break our hearts with the things that break your heart. Fill us with grace to extend hospitality to all, and the courage to live and serve selflessly. Grant us generous hearts to fellowship with each other at your table. Amen!

JESUS BLESSES CHILDREN

Hyacinth Stevens (United States)

MARK 10:13–16

v. 16 *Then he hugged the children and blessed them.*

My church, a former Jewish synagogue, sits in the middle of a densely populated New York City block in the Bronx. This city block has five-story apartment buildings and two-story row houses on both sides of the street. One side of the street is bookended with a mini market or, as we say in the Bronx, the "corner store" or bodega. The other side of the street is occupied by a mid-size supermarket and a small community garden. An estimated four hundred families live within this city block, representing more than twenty countries and nationalities.

On a Sunday morning in mid-July, our congregation had a shortened service as we planned to go out into our community with a mobile prayer station, words of encouragement on scripture cards, and water bottles customized with our church name and mission.

Our goal was to share the love of Christ. The worship service was full of energy and excitement. Like Jesus, we were going out on a mission—we were responding to the "great commission"!

For some time already we had been doing prayer walks in our community. Members were encouraged to make every walk on the street of the church a time of prayer and mindfulness for the community. Prayer walking the block was intended to make our church more aware and responsive to our neighbors, loving and engaging our neighbors as ourselves.

As the congregation's pastor, I would encourage members with statements like: Instead of being frustrated with how far your parking spot is from the church, use the extra steps to pray for the community, or use the long walk from the train station as a time to pray for the community. I was confident that this was our church's big impact summer—we would go out, invite the people, and the church would be filled.

Well, that's not quite how things turned out. A few months later, still looking for fruit from the summer mission, I took my curiosity to my prayer closet. "Lord of the harvest, where is it? You sent, and we went. But where is the harvest? A few new people have come, but Lord, we put in so much effort, gave out lots of water, scriptures, and encouragement. What do we have to show for it?"

Later the same day, while heading to the church, I saw that there was an influx of children on the block despite it being the time when school let out for the day. That day, I was aware of the children and youth in the community in a slightly different way. As they walked with bookbags, some in school uniforms, others not, I was reminded of my prayer from earlier in the day—"Lord of the Harvest, where is it?" Almost instantly, I noticed a middle schooler who occasionally came to church along with her best friend. She was in a vigorous conversation with a group of boys who seemed to be disturbing her. I walked by and greeted her and the boys. My presence at the moment was to check in—to make sure that things were okay and that the heated conversation did not escalate. As I stood in their midst, I sensed the echoing as though God was answering my prayer—this is the harvest!

A few days later, my father, who had been a pastor for over thirty years, asked me about my ministry. So I started sharing.

"It's interesting that you should ask, Dad, because I'm feeling perplexed. We've been doing lots of outreach to the community, mostly to adults, which is good. However, the parents constantly ask what we have to offer the children. And this is where they want the conversation to stay. As I try to ask about them and their needs, it comes back to their children.

"Dad," I said, "I was already a youth minister. I thought pastoring would have a different focus."

He invited me to ponder. "How are children and youth connected to the kingdom? What might you learn that is transferable for the adults? Jesus blesses their children, and the church blesses the children."

Jesus' training moment in Mark 10:13–16 was exactly what Dad was trying to get me to think about. The parents are sending their children to be blessed. Could it be that they recognized that an encounter with Jesus through their children would change their families, their community, and their culture? What the disciples thought was a distraction from the Jesus ministry was actually very significant. Jesus was inviting them to shift from a monocultural mindset, which limits who belongs in the culture. Jesus was modeling an intercultural perspective. "Let them come! Yes, the children belong to the kingdom; and my kingdom belongs to them." I can imagine the murmuring and whispers among the followers of Jesus—these children? Yes, the kingdom is like them: those who are nimble, loving, courageous, willing, available, still growing, and wanting to come to Jesus.

Bless our children, let them come!

During that season of prayer and outreach, the harvest was the children who brought their families to church, who grew and became mentors in the community by working as tutors and program directors in our church's after-school program. Some became leaders in various ministries of the church. Lord, bless our children! The young lady with a group of boys who caught my attention by the Holy Spirit's unction recently completed a medical degree. She is passionate about community-based wellness and health care, and she gives God the praise and cites her faith community as a major supporter. Jesus has blessed her.

For reflection

1. How are the children in your community being blessed?

2. How is Jesus inviting you today to become like a child?

3. Are there hindrances (people, places, and things) to you getting close to Jesus? What are they, and how can you get past them? Can others support you?

Prayer

Bless them, the hearts who want to know you.
Bless them, the minds that desire renewal.
Bless them, the lives that want to be transformed.
Bless them, the ones afraid, pushed away, and isolated.
Bless them, those who wander looking for hope.
Bless them, those came to be touched and blessed by you, Jesus.
Bless us like a child.
Bless us with the wisdom to desire your presence, to be
    close, nimble,
    beaming with the joy of your love, trusting and abiding,
    for theirs is the kingdom.
Bless us, amen.

JESUS ANNOUNCES GOOD NEWS TO THE POOR

Jeremiah Choi (Hong Kong)

LUKE 4:16–30

vv. 18–19 NIV *"The Spirit of the Lord is on me, because he has anointed me to proclaim good news to the poor. He has sent me to proclaim freedom for the prisoners and recovery of sight for the blind, to set the oppressed free, to proclaim the year of the Lord's favor."*

These words of Jesus in Luke 4:16–30 focused the calling I received in 1989. I have been serving Jesus in the Mennonite churches in Hong Kong ever since. Hope Mennonite Church—the third church established by Mennonite missionaries—was born on June 4, 1989, with the baptism of its first two members. I was then employed by the church part-time while also pursuing my studies at the China Bible Seminary.

One might think of Hong Kong as a rich place. However, there are about 1 million poor people among Hong Kong's 7.5 million citizens. The mission of Hope is to spread the gospel among these people—"to proclaim good news to the poor" in Hong Kong.

Agape Mennonite Church, the first Mennonite church in Hong Kong, was formally established in 1976. However, the story started in 1950 when Mennonite Central Committee came to Hong Kong to offer basic assistance to the new immigrants coming from mainland China. At that time, Hong Kong was a relatively small town of five hundred thousand people. But when China became a communist country in 1949, many people left the country and went to Hong Kong. So the population of Hong Kong expanded very rapidly in only a few years.

When it started in 1976, Agape Mennonite Church was located in a government housing estate designed to house poor people. So we can read the heart of the missionaries who have come to Hong Kong—they came "to proclaim good news to the poor."

What does it mean to "to proclaim good news to the poor"? It means you can't expect sufficient financial support from the members. It means you can't expect strong or sustained leadership from the members, who are preoccupied with putting food on the table. It means it will take a long time for a church to grow into a self-sustainable organization. Indeed, the Mennonite churches in Hong Kong have struggled with limited resources, especially after the last missionaries left in 2008. This is not a complaint. The Hong Kong churches deeply appreciate the long-term commitment and efforts of the missionaries, and it was time for the local churches to be independent and to walk on their own.

Some have described Hong Kong as a chess piece between China and the United States. From this perspective, there is no hope of peace in the coming decades. Since July of 1997, when Great Britain officially transferred control of Hong Kong to China, Hong Kong has been under a "one country, two systems" policy. China is a communist government, while Hong Kong, despite lacking strong democratic structures, continues to embrace many of the core values held and practiced by democratic countries. During the past few years, the Chinese government has taken steps to rule Hong Kong more tightly, seeking to resume total control. For this reason, many people are leaving Hong Kong, with some churches losing a significant number of members.

So our circumstances here do not seem to favor the church. What should we do? Should we leave? Should we quit?

"The Spirit of the Lord is on me, because he has anointed me." This was true of Jesus, and it is also true of us—the body of Jesus, his church.

Among other challenges, Agape Church struggled for a long time with the high rental rates of Hong Kong properties. We needed to pay $2,500 monthly for a seven-hundred-square-foot apartment where forty people could gather for worship. Six years ago, God answered our prayer and led us to a school that was willing to rent space for Sunday worship at a lower rate. We believe that we should proclaim good news to the poor, including the many people in the government estate near this school. And Hope Church should also continue its ministry among the marginalized people in their area.

Last year I retired from my full-time job as a pastor. Not long before my retirement, I discovered a problem with an irregular heart rate, perhaps as a prolonged effect of COVID-19. I needed to take medicines for almost a year. I prayed and asked the Lord whether I should stop working after my retirement or continue to work for the church. Around Easter, I fasted and prayed for twenty days. After ten days of fasting I found that my heart problem was gone. Hallelujah! Jesus answered my prayer. He healed me!

This answer to prayer was not only a healing of my body; it also means that I can continue to extend care to Christ's body—the church. If Jesus is on our side, then nothing can stop us from serving him.

For reflection

1. Jesus faced unfriendly situations; how does this passage inspire you in your situation?

2. "The Spirit of the Lord is on me, because he has anointed me." What do these words mean to you?

3. Who are your neighbors? What are you doing for them in the name of Jesus?

Prayer

"The Spirit of the Lord is on me, because he has anointed me." Therefore, we need not fear. May the Spirit of the Lord continue to guide the Hong Kong churches and help them proclaim good news to the poor. May all churches around the world trust in Jesus as their provider. Amen.

JESUS CHALLENGES HIS FOLLOWERS TO FULL COMMITMENT

Samson Omondi Ongode (Kenya)

LUKE 9:57–62

---

vv. 60–62 *Jesus said to him, "Let the dead bury their own dead. But you go and spread the news of God's kingdom." Someone else said to Jesus, "I will follow you, Lord, but first let me say good-bye to those in my house." Jesus said to him, "No one who puts a hand on the plow and looks back is fit for God's kingdom."*

This passage reminds us of the dilemma we face when Jesus challenges our seemingly reasonable excuses by exposing their superficial nature and the way they mask the true desires of our heart. In each of the examples we see potential Christ-followers held up by fear, insecurity, and a lack of understanding. The scripture does not reveal their final decision. Instead, it focuses on their original reaction since what comes to mind first typically reveals the heart.

Make no mistake. The path of righteousness is a hard and narrow road. But to the one who is willing to trust in God's sovereignty, a transformation of the heart is possible if we answer "Yes, Lord" by faith rather than defaulting to the excuses that blind our hearts and reveal our lack of trust in Jesus Christ.

The challenge many have with Luke 9:57–62 is that it seems abrasive—even cold and unloving. After all, the excuses are relatively reasonable, just tempting enough to brush past them quickly without the slightest consideration. However, when we look closer at Jesus' response to each potential follower we realize that we are similarly guilty of rationalizing our own behaviors in order to sidestep the personal responsibility and sacrifice that are part of Christian discipleship.

We shouldn't dismiss the superficial desires of these followers' hearts as disingenuous. It would appear that they sincerely desired to follow Jesus. Yet their superficiality becomes apparent when Jesus unexpectedly counters their excuses not with conditions but with accountability.

The real identity of a disciple is found in our willingness to die to self for the sake of the gospel. Paul reminds us, "Don't be conformed to the patterns of this world, but be transformed by the renewing of your minds so that you can figure out what God's will is—what is good and pleasing and mature" (Romans 12:2). Our minds will never be renewed if they are cut off from hearing the truth of God's Word; excuses thrive in an environment where accountability is absent.

The rebuke Jesus offers paints a clear picture of what real discipleship means—namely, a willingness to embrace poverty, hardship, and persecution if that should be God's will. Put another way, followers of Jesus have no guarantees that their lives will be comfortable. To the contrary. It is sobering to realize how self-protecting we often become when faced with adversity or when we are held accountable to God's Word. Yet accountability can actually be a blessing if we embrace it and apply it. For example, I sometimes find it very difficult and challenging to endure the hardships of ministry, especially when I am forced to travel by public bus in order to visit congregations that are spread all over the country. Nonetheless, God's grace is sufficient to carry me through the activities.

Therefore, before we proclaim our willingness to follow Jesus Christ wherever he would go, we are wise to consider the cost of what it means to be a disciple of Jesus Christ and then to compare that to the price Jesus Christ paid on the cross for our sins. Naturally we will realize how priceless a gift we have been offered for no other reason except love.

Priorities may easily become complicated since many of us assume our family comes first. In this passage Jesus is not contradicting biblical obligations regarding our families. But if our family becomes an idol in our hearts, drawing us away from loving God first and foremost, then we must address our priorities. God must always come before our spouses, and our spouses before our children since they are the offspring of marriage. Jesus was not being insensitive to the potential follower's desire to bury his father. But note that the man's excuse included no timetable. Prolonging or putting off a decision to follow Jesus Christ assumes we will have life and breath in the future to make such decisions. This presumption that we can foretell the future reveals our weakness. At the same time, it also exposes what comes first in our hearts.

In the end, this passage reminds us that placing anything or anyone before God will always become a divisive wedge in our faith walk if we accept it.

For reflection

1. What excuses are you tempted to put forward that may be keeping you from a fuller commitment to following Jesus?

2. Are you holding tightly to something in your past—perhaps forgiveness for sins for which you have already repented—that blinds you from looking forward?

Prayer

Almighty Father, I adore you and uplift your name. Help us to identify and prioritize our purpose in life, which is ultimately to serve you and others in and out of season. Guide us, Lord, so that we might navigate through our difficult and trying moments to serve you and others more completely, amidst poverty, hardship, and persecution, without compromising your Word. Amen.

JESUS TEACHES ABOUT THE NARROW WAY

Kkot-Ip Bae (South Korea)

LUKE 13:22–30

---

v. 24 *"Make every effort to enter through the narrow gate. Many, I tell you, will try to enter and won't be able to."*

For those who have traveled to Korea, or as a Korean traveling abroad, one of the most surprising aspects of Korean culture might be the fact that if you happen to forget your wallet, laptop, or phone in a public place—be it a café, restaurant, or even on the streets—nobody will take it. A wallet dropped in an elevator remains untouched. A phone forgotten in the restroom is still there when you return. People confidently leave their belongings on café tables while using the restroom. While the presence of high-performance CCTV cameras and the threat of a swift police response might play a role in this, most Koreans have internalized a strong moral value against taking what isn't theirs.

Yet, ironically, many Koreans often feel like something of value is constantly being taken from our lives.

Korea has seen a whirlwind of historical events in a short period: the Japanese occupation (1910 to 1945); the sudden emergence of democracy due to the Korean War (1950 to 1953); a political whiplash from dictatorships to democratization movements; rapid economic growth in the 1980s and early 1990s followed by the IMF economic crisis in 1997. With few natural resources like oil, Korea's survival in the global market has relied on developing its human resources. However, this context has created a sense of fierce competition in Korean society; and as the competition intensified, the wealth gap has widened. Behind the glitz of K-pop and K-drama lies a darker reality: among the thirty-eight member countries of the Organization for Economic Co-operation and Development (OECD), Korea ranks the highest for suicide rates, gender wage gaps, elderly poverty rates, low birth rates, and industrial accident mortality rates.

In the scripture text for today, Jesus speaks about the "narrow gate." Young people in Korea today face numerous narrow gates including competition for acceptance in the prestigious universities in Seoul, employment at a major corporation, and marrying into wealth or access to family wealth. In a society where everyone is fiercely competing against each other, these doors can often seem very narrow. Students study for fifteen hours a day. Workers work overtime until dawn. People speculate in stocks, cryptocurrencies, and real estate in pursuit of stability and wealth. Everyone competes to enter these doors because that's deemed the right path, the path of a winner in society. In such a society, poverty is evidence of individual failure—almost a sin. Those who fail to enter these doors become losers.

With a sociology degree, I've been actively involved in various social issues, including work with a Christian youth nonprofit organization engaged in anti-poverty initiatives. As part of that work, I've stood by those displaced by gentrification, those forced to relocate from their hometowns due to government policies, and workers who risk their lives due to hazardous working conditions. Together, we have worshiped, protested, prayed, and raised our voices. Though the circumstances varied, we shared the same poverty . . . and the same pain.

It was also on those cold streets where I met Jesus—the same Jesus who walked this earth taking the form of a poor person, siding with those who were weak, vulnerable, and at the edges of society.

The efforts I have witnessed in Korea of people striving to enter through society's narrow doors contrast starkly with Jesus' invitation to follow him through the path of his "narrow gate." Society's doors are sought by many, whereas almost no one desires to enter Jesus' narrow door. Standing before Jesus' narrow door, the impulse is to turn away, to flee. Who willingly walks into poverty? Yet I have taken one step at a time toward that door, because I want to follow his path.

The best way to endure, to avoid turning back, is to join hands with the community. Our church community cares for our neighbors. We stand with those in need. We talk about opposing war and making peace, even though many don't want to hear it. Despite discomfort, we speak out against plans to build a factory producing weapons of destruction near our church.

We're not opening the world's doors; instead, we have chosen this narrow path.

For reflection

---

1. What narrow doors exist in your country?

2. If Jesus is for the poor, what does it mean to follow in his footsteps?

3. As an Anabaptist, how do you strive to enter Jesus' narrow door?

Prayer

Make us poor.
Take everything we have.
Lead us on the path of your great defeat. Amen.

Part 6

ON THE ROAD TO JERUSALEM

THE UNSETTLING MESSAGE OF JESUS

Vikal Pravin Rao (India)

LUKE 12:51–53

> **v. 51** *"Do you think that I have come to bring peace to the earth? No, I tell you, I have come instead to bring division."*

In this passage, Jesus poses an interesting question . . . and offers a surprising—even perplexing—response. "Do you think that I have come to give peace on earth?" he asks. The answer is actually "No." Indeed, Jesus insists that he has come to bring division, which he says will become evident even within individual households.

Jesus came to bring peace between God and humans, but only if we accept his work on the cross and the transformation of life that follows. The crucial point here is that our choice to accept Jesus and follow in his way has consequences—it will change how we live our daily lives. Sometimes, this new way of life will naturally lead to tensions with society around us and even tensions within our own households. That's what Jesus means here when he says, "Do you think I came to bring peace?"

India is a multicultural, multilingual, multiethnic, multireligious society where Christianity is a minority religion. As followers of Jesus, our faith is challenged every day. Christians in India are required to attend certain national and religious festivals in our workplaces, where we are expected to participate in rituals that are contrary to our personal faith.

There are many examples in my community where one or two members of a family are Christians, but the rest are not. It is not uncommon for nonbelieving family members to persecute Christians, sometimes in very aggressive ways. Christians, for example, are sometimes deprived of basic human needs such as access to water from local wells or the public water supply, or not allowed to enter local shops, or compelled to flee their homes, or not permitted to bury their dead. At times, those hostile to Christians have even set their personal possessions, homes, or entire villages on fire.

In addition, there is a strong social expectation in India that all family members will attend certain social gatherings hosted by people of various religious persuasions. If you are part of polite society, it is assumed that you will attend these gatherings and accept whatever belief system is being represented. Sometimes the family puts a great deal of pressure on believers to participate. In many families, members who believe in Jesus are afraid to openly acknowledge their faith because they would lose their standing in their family. There are numerous stories of persecution within the family.

Yet we feel that participating in pagan rituals, celebrations, and observances is a compromise of our personal faith in Jesus Christ. This is what Jesus is talking about when he says, "Don't think that I have come to bring peace."

In some situations where believers and nonbelievers live alongside each other in the intimacy of a household, Jesus' presence is going to cause division. The division Jesus is talking about in this passage occurs because of the reality of truth. Jesus is the personification of the truth. Jesus said, "I am the way, the truth, and the life" (John 14:6). By its very nature, the truth of Jesus divides—there will always be people who embrace truth and those people who reject it.

The truth embodied by Jesus helps us to stand firm in our beliefs, regardless of our daily circumstances. Truth helps a believer to judge what is right on our part. The living Word of God teaches the truth. As Jesus said, "And you will know the truth, and the truth will make you free" (John 8:32 NRSVue).

There will be divisions, but Jesus promises that the truth will set us free.

For reflection

1. We often imagine Jesus as a gentle shepherd who brings peace and reconciliation. Does this passage change your perception of Jesus?

2. Have you ever experienced division in your family or community because of your faith? If so, how did you respond?

3. What does Jesus' claim that he is "the way, the truth, and the life" mean to you?

Prayer

Oh Lord, help us to stay firm in our convictions, to share the truth freely with others, and to show your love to those who would do us harm. Amen.

JESUS' TRIUMPHAL ENTRY INTO JERUSALEM

Atsuhiro Katano (Japan)

MARK 11:1–11

v. 9 *"Hosanna! Blessings on the one who comes in the name of the Lord!"*

This passage, the story of Jesus' entry into Jerusalem, poses a challenge to the Japanese cultural understandings of leadership.

Mark's gospel begins with the story of Jesus' baptism in the Jordan River. Then he proclaims the kingdom of God, makes disciples, and calls for repentance through his teachings and miracles. Jesus came to embody the reign of God. He came as the one who would save them. Now Jesus is moving toward Jerusalem, fully aware of his own imminent suffering, death, . . . and resurrection (Mark 10:32–34).

In this text, Jesus tells the disciples to prepare for his entry, in line with the prophecy of Zechariah (Zechariah 9:9), who envisioned the entry of a messianic king who is righteous, victorious, and humble. Just as the prophet foretold, the people responded joyfully, welcoming him "in the name of the Lord!" (Mark 11:9).

The reality that followed, however, was radically different from what people were expecting of a messianic king. Before his entry, Jesus healed the sick, cast out demons, and reached out to the marginalized. Now, after entering Jerusalem, he seems to put more emphasis on challenging authority, confronting injustices, and warning people with prophecies about the end time.

Neither the disciples nor the people in Jerusalem understood that Jesus came to save them not as a military hero but through his suffering, death, and resurrection. They were first shocked, then disappointed, and then resentful. Those who had joyfully welcomed Jesus as a liberator into Jerusalem soon turned into "the crowd" who shouted for his crucifixion.

Japan is famous for its high-context culture. Here, social norms tend to be generated collectively, with behavioral expectations highly dependent on the sentiment of the majority. People here tend to perceive society as homogeneous, where members share a common history, common virtues, and common sensibilities. Differences are tolerated, but only if the collective foundation is not challenged. The Anabaptist commitment to nonviolence, for example, is generally admired by most people (whether Christians or not)—until, that is, our pacifism disturbs the existing social harmony by seeking justice through nonviolent resistance.

The Japanese Mennonite Church is no exception. My wife serves as non-salaried pastor of a Mennonite house church with fifteen baptized members. She once asked the congregation to establish a specific job description for her ministry. On the face of it, it seems like it should not be hard for a small group of people to clarify what they expect of a pastor. However, in Japan the role of "pastor" is understood primarily as a rank or status, rather than an occupation with clearly-defined tasks. Thus, members were reluctant, if not outright resistant, to describe her role in terms of specific assignments. Members were uncomfortable with a church polity in which leadership roles were defined in terms of a contract. They preferred to describe the role of pastor as "taking care of the whole," leaving the meaning of "care" and "whole" ambiguous, depending on the situation.

In such a context, even the community of faith seems to turn into a highly traditional family, where the housewife is expected to handle all of the chores associated with "housework" without the details of keeping track of hours, an office schedule, or a retirement plan. The church has set up its own context and nobody is qualified to change it.

What would it look like if Jesus entered my high-context church? He would not ride in a limousine, but would probably walk from the nearest bus stop. No doubt the church members would stand in line, greeting him joyfully, and warmly welcoming him to the worship hall.

But I am afraid that we would do this with our own distorted expectations of a messianic king. We would likely welcome Jesus only if he conformed to our context. Nobody would dare to ask him what, exactly, he came to accomplish in our church. For our own peace of mind, we might project our own favorite assumptions regarding a Savior. Reluctant to clarify details, we might optimistically assume that our Savior should simply be nice to us, setting aside his own will in order to preserve a sense of peace within the community. Indeed, we might end up feeling disappointed or even betrayed by who he really is.

Nonconformity is an ongoing challenge to Anabaptists living in high-context settings.

For reflection

1. Many Christians seem to prefer the joyful shouts of "Hosanna" to the uncomfortable challenges Jesus poses to our assumptions about security and power. If you were to welcome Jesus into your church today, what do you think he would say?

2. What does nonconformity mean in your context?

Prayer

Lord, you come to us in our own contexts. You come to the center of our culture's understanding of power and authority . . . to the center of our yearnings, aspirations, and hidden agenda. Lord, break down the defensive walls in our hearts; challenge our distorted image of you. Give us wisdom and courage to call into question our own understandings, so that we may grow in faithfulness and become more Christ-like. Make the light of truth shine on us so that our preoccupations might be transformed into deeper knowledge and more faithful practice. Lord, have mercy on us. Amen.

JESUS INSTITUTES THE MEAL OF REMEMBRANCE

Sindah Ngulube (Zimbabwe)

LUKE 22:14–20

v. 19 *After taking the bread and giving thanks, he broke it and gave it to them, saying, "This is my body, which is given for you. Do this in remembrance of me."*

If only we had made it on time, we would be eating rice and chicken like the other guests," she lamented. We were traveling to a wedding in my hometown of Bulawayo. As a minister, I had the responsibility of officiating at multiple weddings that day and I had brought my daughters and their friends along on the journey. Regrettably, however, we somehow missed all the lunchtime receptions. By the time we reached the final wedding, lunch had long been served and the food put away. It was at this moment that my daughter's friend expressed how disheartened she was.

Life often surprises us with disappointments. Like my daughter's friend who was eagerly anticipating a meal of rice and chicken, there are many times when our material expectations are not fulfilled.

Yet God calls us to find contentment in him. Reflecting on the Last Supper, where Jesus declared, "I am the bread of life" (John 6:35), we learn that true fulfillment lies in seeking him alone. Bread sustains physical life; Jesus sustains spiritual life. The bread that Jesus broke and shared with his disciples represents the body of Christ that was broken for us (Luke 22:19). Just as we need daily bread for our bodies, we need Jesus for our souls. The wine Jesus shared symbolizes both joy and suffering. It represents the blood of the new covenant, sealing God's promise of redemption (Matthew 26:17–29). Together, the bread and wine signify the intimate connection between Jesus' sacrifice and our salvation.

Here, in the final hours before his death, Jesus is the provider. One of the names of God in the Old Testament is Jehovah Jireh (Hebrew "to provide," or "God, the provider"). God provides for our emotional, spiritual, and physical needs. He is a God who provides security in a country that is riddled with economic difficulties and challenges that frequently seem to be beyond human repair.

I call on Jehovah Jireh because I know I can count on God's grace and provision, which is enough for me. He is Jehovah Jireh because he takes away the lie of self-sufficiency—we cannot exist apart from God. Jehovah Jireh provides for my family. Jehovah Jireh provides for my church. He sustains my spiritual and emotional needs. He provides protection and spiritual cover in moments of need.

I call God Jehovah Jireh because he is a father who loves us.

Yes, there are times when we are disappointed in our expectations. There are perhaps even times when we are physically hungry. But Jesus as the bread of life invites us to partake in his divine presence, to find nourishment for our souls, and to remember his sacrificial love.

For reflection

1. What excuses might be holding you back from accepting Jesus' invitation to join him at the table so you can experience his love? Think of the shortcomings of the disciples he served at the Last Supper.

2. In what areas of your life have you experienced God being Jehovah Jireh, the provider?

Prayer

Dear heavenly Father, the creator of the heavens and the earth: Thank you for your grace and your sacrificial love for us! Thank you for providing us with the gift of life. I intercede for every heart that seeks to know you and every soul that desires to have a relationship with you. Reveal yourself in ways that these hearts and minds can comprehend. Heavenly Father, I also pray that you remind us to rely confidently on you. In every circumstance, remind us that we cannot exist without you and that this life you gave us is yours. Help us to lead selfless lives and to commit to the great commission, which is to make disciples of all nations. Lead us to the cross for redemption and repentance, and help us to live a life of holiness, for it is because of your sacrifice that we can look forward to eternity. May the grace of our Lord Jesus Christ and the love of God the Father and the fellowship of the Holy Spirit be with you all. In the name of our Lord and Savior, Jesus Christ. Amen!

JESUS' FAREWELL TO HIS DISCIPLES

Wieteke van der Molen (Netherlands)

JOHN 14:1–16:33

v. 1 *"Don't be troubled. Trust in God. Trust also in me."*

As we sit in silence, we light a candle. We stare into the gentle golden light, remembering the light of the world. We gaze into each other's eyes, remembering Christ's humanity, recognizing him in our own humanity. We tell stories and testimonies of how his teachings have been relevant in our lives, our relationships, and the world around us. We sing, grateful for life itself and life as followers of Jesus. And we sit in silent wonderment to be part of it all. To just be.

The setting in which we live and work—a Mennonite retreat center known as Dopersduin, located in the dunes of the northern seacoast of the Netherlands—is a gentle place in a harsh and individualized world. In our cultural context, Christianity is mostly seen as a slightly embarrassing relic of the past. There are not a lot of Christians in our highly individualized and secularized environment. Everything and everyone around us tells us that we should move beyond childish beliefs or get over religious illusions.

But then here is this house, this place. Gentle and welcoming. Not of this world, but determinedly of his world. We have no real mission other than to simply be here and hold this space for the Spirit to work. Dopersduin is a foothold of gentleness in a hardening world. People open up here. They find something that is often lost in other settings. They soften. They get curious. I like to think it is the Spirit working, showing us the Way.

The text of John 14:1–16:33 (CEV) reads like a prayer to me; indeed, it almost sings. Certain lines jump out as if highlighted by the Spirit. Together they form a song of encouragement:

> Don't be worried! (14:1)
> I am the way, the truth, and the life! (14:6)
> You are already clean because of what I have said to you. (15:3)
> Let my teachings become part of you. (15:7)
> Remain faithful to my love for you. (15:9)
> I tell you to love each other, as I have loved you. (15:12)
> I command you to love each other! (15:17)
> You will be (so/completely) happy. (16:20, 21, 22, 24)
> Cheer up! (16:33)

These words sing to my soul. They speak of truth and faith, of love and joy, of living the Way. They offer a way of life in the path of Jesus. Nothing in this text is self-righteous or too big. Instead, we encounter a gentle soul-searching. Here are teachings that can become part of who I am; who we are. Here are guidelines for deep and devout love. A love so present and vibrant that it will live forever. It cannot die.

So who cares what the world thinks? Who cares if we are considered old-fashioned or irrelevant? Even if we, in the end, cannot hold out—even if we disappear—I am not worried. Jesus is right. There is nothing to worry about.

Living the Way is not about growing in numbers or power. But neither is it about dwindling numbers or ridicule. Instead, it is an invitation to live with grace, gentleness, and love. And when we fail, we are invited to try again and again. We are not heroes. We are simple folk, with simple lives. Living in the Way is an ongoing practice, day after day.

So yes, we sit. We light a candle. We sing, share, and pray. We listen in silence. We try not to fear. We are attentive to the Love that will never die.

We are not worried . . . well, mostly we are not worried!

For reflection

1. What themes from this devotional speak to your experience?

2. What words from this passage "sing to your soul"?

3. "Living the Way is . . . an invitation to live with grace, gentleness, and love." How have you experienced this?

Prayer

May you always be fearless in the love of our Lord, knowing that it is there for you; you just have to let it be. No judgment, no harshness, no shame, no fear.

May that love help you find your way through life, knowing that you are already clean, for he has told you so. No judgment, no harshness, no shame, no fear.

May his teachings become part of you, lifting you up in the knowledge that he flows through you, always recreating you. No judgment, no harshness, no shame, no fear.

May his love transform you—loving, gentle, and vibrant. May you know the world in a different way, seeing it as he does, without judgment, harshness, shame, or fear.

May your love help to carry the stories and worries of others. May your love show your people a different way of life, without judgment, harshness, shame, or fear.

May you be joyful as he promised, knowing life is a beautiful, generous gift.

Cheer up! Cheer up! Cheer up!

JESUS IS CRUCIFIED

Neal Blough (France)

MARK 15:16–39

---

v. 39 *When the centurion, who stood facing Jesus, saw how he died, he said, "This man was certainly God's Son."*

The portrayal of the crucifixion in Mark's gospel describes the mockery and humiliation that preceded Jesus' death by extreme torture. It also tells of the mockery Jesus experienced on the cross as he was dying in great pain. How do we move from the awfulness and horror of this death to faith in the living Christ?

All four Gospels lead up to—and provide the context for under-standing—Jesus' death and resurrection. In these narratives we clearly see the down-to-earth reality of the incarnation. God came into the world with self-giving love, even unto death in the face of evil. Our faith proclaims this terrible death, followed by the resurrection, as the source of salvation. Through these events, evil, sin, and death are defeated. Forgiveness and new life become a reality.

Nevertheless, the cross can be misunderstood. The first time Jesus announced his coming death in Mark's gospel, "Peter took hold of Jesus and, scolding him, began to correct him" (Matthew 16:22). Jesus' response to the disciples' refusal of a crucified Messiah was "take up your cross and follow me." The cross is both the source of salvation, and our model and means for confronting life, especially evil.

Following Jesus is not something we can do on our own strength. After the cross and the resurrection came Pentecost. The outpouring of the Spirit offered the possibility of experiencing the living Christ as well as bearing the fruit of a transformed life.

Throughout my life, I have been aware of the presence of the living Christ in many ways. These have included prayer, studying Scripture, sharing experiences with family members, participating in congregational life and in larger church contexts (Mennonite and other), as well as all of the many difficult and joyful experiences that life has to offer. All of this has been reinforced by years of participating in two multicultural congregations in Paris. In those settings, I have regularly experienced a mixture of African, Caribbean, and European spirituality, music, and worship styles. It has also meant learning how to live together despite the French colonial past, as well as the economic and racial injustice suffered by many church members still today.

On any given Sunday morning, participants in worship frequently offer spontaneous songs of thanksgiving for the salvation that comes from the cross, or prayers for forgiveness, for healing, and for the possibility of a new life. At the same time, the prayer requests coming from the countries of origin of our church members (including Haiti, Cameroon, the two Congos, and Ivory Coast) reflect a strong awareness of sin, injustice, and oppression. Songs of African origin have become part of the worship experience, and often include a call to discipleship: "walking in the light of God," "we walk his way," "I want to walk beside my Lord."

The meaning of the cross can be misconstrued by an exclusive emphasis on personal salvation with no mention of discipleship or community. That is not what is seen in the Gospels or the epistles; nor is it present in the origins of Anabaptism. The early Anabaptist theme of discipleship contained a strong emphasis on the cross, both as the source of salvation and as a way of living.

But from immigrant sisters and brothers, I have also learned that to see the cross only as a model of life or a source of ethics is to minimize the reality of sin in our own lives and to downgrade the importance of repentance. It is possible to truly follow Jesus only when we see our own need of salvation and come to understand that discipleship is not something we can do from our own strength.

For reflection

1. When you read the dramatic details of this passage, what stands out most vividly for you? Why?

2. How would you explain the crucifixion and resurrection to a non-Christian friend? Why is this story so important to the Christian life?

3. How have you experienced the presence of the living Christ in your life?

Prayer

We give you thanks, Lord, that you so loved the world, your creation, that you came to live among us. On the cross, you took upon yourself the consequences of evil, thereby defeating sin and death, giving us the possibility of new life as we follow Jesus in the power of your Spirit. We also give thanks for the five hundred years of history that has shaped our family, and for the privilege of being a worldwide family that can be enriched by the gifts and perspectives of all.

Part 7

RESURRECTION

JESUS IS RESURRECTED

Henk Stenvers (Netherlands)

MATTHEW 28:1–10

---

vv. 5–6 *"Don't be afraid. I know that you are looking for Jesus who was crucified. He isn't here, because he's been raised from the dead, just as he said."*

The shocking week of the crucifixion is now over. Following the Sabbath, a new week has begun, and with it the dawn of a new era. How well we can relate to the women who are visiting Jesus' tomb. Tending the fresh grave of a loved one reflects a deep human need to hold on to memories of the departed, as if we are somehow still together. Visiting the cemetery is a way of dealing with the sense of unreality associated with death—"Has this really happened?" we ask ourselves. Maybe it was all a bad dream.

But then the whole situation changes dramatically. God intervenes in a shocking way. An earthquake, followed by the dramatic appearance of an angel, paralyzes the guards so that "they became like dead men" (Matthew 28:4). The weapons of the world, it would seem, cannot stop this heavenly intervention.

The women must have been terrified by these frightening developments. But the angel says to them, "Don't be afraid." Jesus, the angel informs them, has risen from the dead. Now they should quickly go to his disciples and tell them to meet Jesus in Galilee.

Filled with a complicated mixture of incredulity, fear, and joy, the women can scarcely believe what is happening. But as they run from the grave, they encounter the resurrected Jesus. They touch his feet. It is really his body. And again they hear the words: "Don't be afraid." Almost instantly, the despair they felt following the crucifixion is transformed into wonder and renewed hope.

We do not encounter Jesus in this physical way. But Jesus did give us the Spirit, and we can trust that wherever we experience the Spirit among us, Jesus is present.

Recently I joined a team from Dnipro Hope Mission, a small NGO that supports Ukrainian Baptist and Mennonite pastors, to see firsthand the work they are doing for the poor in that war-torn country. I live in the Netherlands, one of the most prosperous countries in Europe. In my country, the war in Ukraine is both very close and exceedingly distant. On the one hand, we hear horrifying stories and see images of violence and destruction in vivid color on TV. But at the same time that violence seems very far from the reality of daily Dutch life. Frequently, it seems that all we can do is to offer a small bit of help in the form of money and relief goods, or by promising to keep the pastors and all those who suffer from war in our prayers.

Soon after the initial invasion by the Russian army in 2022, the work of the pastors changed dramatically. Almost overnight, waves of refugees began to pass by their churches. Since then, the regular messages we receive from Mennonite Brethren pastors tell stories of hunger, suffering, and death.

The pastors have been working day and night, offering a safe place for refugees to eat, rest, and shower, before they continue on their way. The pastors also began to reach out to those who had been left behind in small towns and villages, providing them with food, clothes, and spiritual support, even as they risked their lives on a daily basis. Their courageous and sacrificial actions brought a bit of hope to a hopeless situation.

Our visit to the pastors was meant as an act of solidarity. The Dnipro Hope Mission team invited the pastors, along with their spouses, to gather together in a safe part of Ukraine, giving them a few days away from the stress and danger to rest and share with each other.

For three days, we listened to their stories, sharing our laments and prayers, and remembering together the loss of so many innocent lives. The trauma, pain, and weariness were clearly evident in the eyes of the men and women. On the last evening we read John 13—the story of how Jesus washed the feet of his disciples and called on his disciples to do the same. As we reflected on those words, the Spirit moved us to respond. "We cannot stand in your shoes. But the least we can do is what Jesus did, wash your feet." So our small group knelt and washed the feet of all the people in the room.

Denis Gorenkov, one of the Ukrainian pastors attending the gathering, later wrote: "Those who are involved in humanitarian projects and pastoral care are all too familiar with loneliness, anhedonia, weakness, despondency, cynicism. . . . But all this evaporated as our brothers and sisters washed our feet and dried them with towels."

The brothers and sisters offering pastoral care in Ukraine must wonder where Jesus is in their struggle. But in the room that day we felt the Spirit present among us. In the midst of despair we witnessed new glimmers of hope. We left with a new certainty that Jesus is indeed with the suffering people of Ukraine, and with all those who bear witness to the hungry and needy in the world, or extend the love of Christ in the form of material aid or spiritual support.

The grieving women who came to the grave thought that everything was lost. Yet, to their surprise, they found new hope through an encounter with the living Jesus. So too, our Ukrainian brothers and sisters left the gathering with new hope, knowing that they are not alone, because they encountered the living Christ in the sharing, prayer, and footwashing that we experienced together. They departed the meeting with a glimmer of hope in their eyes.

Jesus is present wherever people express compassion for each other.

For reflection

1. Scripture is filled with phrases like "Fear not" or "Don't be afraid." How does this encouragement become real to you?

2. How have you found hope in the midst of seemingly overwhelming challenges?

3. Has footwashing been a meaningful experience for you? Why or why not?

Prayer

For those who are trying to live under the threat of bombs in the night,
　　For those who had to flee for their lives,
　　For those who are hungry,
　　For those who are mourning the violent death of family and friends,
　　We pray, God, bless them. Jesus be with them!
　　Give hope that the suffering will end.
For those who open their houses and churches,
　　For those who risk their lives to bring food and relief,
　　For those who are your agents in showing your unconditional love,
　　For those who stand with the suffering and dying,
　　We pray, God, bless them. Jesus be with them!
　　Give strength and hope that peace will come!
For those who offer support with money and goods,
　　For those who pray again and again that the wars may end,
　　For those who protest the warmongering of states,
　　For those who are peacemakers in your name,
　　We pray, God bless them, Jesus be with them!
　　May their voices never stop crying out until your kingdom comes.

WITNESSES TO THE RESURRECTION

Rafael Zaracho (Paraguay)

JOHN 20:1–20

v. 18 *Mary Magdalene left and announced to the disciples, "I've seen the Lord." Then she told them what he said to her.*

As a teacher and administrator at Instituto Biblico Asuncíon, a Mennonite Brethren seminary in Paraguay, and as an active member of an urban congregation, I am increasingly convinced that our testimony as Christians depends on the credibility of our communal witness—is our testimony actually convincing or credible?

In John chapter 20, we see three encounters with the resurrected Jesus that can guide us in our role as credible witnesses. The first encounter focuses on Mary Magdalene (20:1–2). As a witness to the resurrected Jesus, Mary Magdalene runs to tell Peter and John that the tomb is empty. The account emphasizes that the two disciples came and that they "saw and believed" (v. 8).

Then Jesus appears again to Mary Magdalene and engages her in a conversation (John 20:14–18). After that encounter Mary Magdalene fulfills her role as a witness: "Mary Magdalene went to the disciples with the news: 'I have seen the Lord!' And she told them that he had said these things to her" (v. 18 NIV). Again and again the text describes Mary Magdalene as a witness, that is, someone who plays a role in communicating what they have seen and experienced.

John then describes a second encounter, this time between the resurrected Jesus and the disciples (20:19–23). The biblical text paints an extremely sad scene, describing a setting in which several of the disciples are hiding in fear. But at the moment when the doors were locked and the disciples were terrified, "Jesus came and stood among them" (John 20:19). As he stood with them, Jesus said, "Peace be with you." The presence of the resurrected Jesus comforted them, providing peace and the assurance of God's continued presence in their midst. We hear a similar echo of this same peace several chapters earlier when Jesus assured the disciples that "The Companion, the Holy Spirit, whom the Father will send in my name, will teach you everything and will remind you of everything I told you. Peace I leave with you. My peace I give you. I give to you not as the world gives. Don't be troubled or afraid" (John 14:26–27). Here the followers of Jesus, as witnesses of his resurrection, are given a model for their own life and mission.

Several chapters later, when Jesus assures his followers: "Peace be with you! As the Father has sent me, I am sending you" (John 20:21 NIV), the emphasis is clearly on sending. This sending has an accent of going out and living among people. And it is in this context of "sending" that Jesus reaffirms his continued presence among his disciples through the Holy Spirit (20:22). The passage closes with the command: "If you forgive anyone's sins, they are forgiven; if you don't forgive them, they aren't forgiven" (20:23). The very nature of this community is one that is sent as a witness to his resurrection. In this process of going—of being sent—the primary task is to offer forgiveness, deliverance, and restoration as modeled by the life and ministry of Jesus.

In the third story we encounter a meeting with Thomas, who was not present when Jesus appeared to the disciples in the previous story. This means that Thomas was the only one who had dared to leave the room—perhaps to fetch food or to carry out some other task. The others were hiding, according to the text, "because they were afraid of the Jewish authorities" (v. 19), worried that they too would be accused and suffer the same fate as their teacher—namely, crucifixion. Thomas returns to the other disciples and hears the news that "We've seen the Lord!" Thomas responds, "Unless I see the nail marks in his hands, put my finger in the wounds left by the nails, and put my hand into his side, I won't believe" (v. 25). At this point we often assume that Thomas was asking for something extra in order to believe. No, Thomas was simply asking to have the same experience as the other ten disciples who had seen Jesus' hands and side and had received Jesus' words of comfort and hope.

The story continues a week later in a setting very similar to the first scene. According to the text, "Even though the doors were locked, Jesus entered and stood among them. He said, 'Peace be with you.'" Then he said to Thomas, "Put your finger here. Look at my hands. Put your hand into my side. No more disbelief. Believe!" (vv. 26–27). Caravaggio's famous painting, "The Incredulity of Saint Thomas," clearly depicts the moment where Jesus grabs Thomas's hand. We could understand this gesture as an attempt to bolster Thomas's belief and to provide a solid basis for his faith. Jesus provides Thomas with what he needs in order to believe. Our God does not invite us to believe without evidence. The gospel of John repeatedly emphasizes that Jesus performed many miracles so that people could believe (20:31).

We do not know how the other ten disciples reacted or what they might have said about their experiences in their first encounter with the resurrected Jesus. But we do know that Thomas responds with faith and trust, affirming "My Lord and my God!" (v. 28). But how are we then to understand Jesus' response: "Do you believe because you see me? Happy are those who don't see and yet believe" (v. 29)? Is this a rebuke to Thomas? Or is it perhaps intended as a rebuke to the ten disciples—the ones who had seen and experienced the presence of the resurrected Christ, but whose testimony was not as convincing as other witnesses of the resurrection because they were still afraid and hiding within the safety of the four walls? Jesus reprimands Thomas for his lack of belief, but perhaps the reprimand was directed even more to the other ten who had seen and experienced the presence of the Risen Lord.

These words are also a wake-up call to all of us who have seen and experienced the presence and power of God in our lives and in the lives of our loved ones. More than a rebuke to Thomas, Jesus is calling each of us to be a community of witnesses that experiences— and helps others to believe in—the resurrected Jesus. Our primary calling is not to accuse the Thomases of today—those who, like us, require a direct encounter with the risen Jesus. Instead, as witnesses we are called first and foremost to examine ourselves and to repent for the many times that we proclaim with the ten disciples that "we have seen the Lord!" while the witness of our lifestyle is marked by superficiality and a disregard towards those in need. We say, "We have seen the Lord!" but we live as if we have not seen "the hands and the side" of the Lord.[5]

This text from John 20 invites us to do what Jesus did—to offer love, mercy, and forgiveness as "proofs" of our role as witnesses of his resurrection. Or as the chapter concludes, "But these things are written so that you will believe that Jesus is the Christ, God's Son, and that believing, you will have life in his name" (v. 31).

For reflection

1. As witnesses of his resurrection how can we make the claims of our faith more credible or convincing?

2. What actions can you take to help others have an encounter with Jesus so they can also believe?

Prayer

As witnesses of your resurrection, help us to proclaim with our voice and our actions that "We have seen the Lord!" May our way of life provide sufficient evidence to people both within and outside our community of faith so that they can affirm that they too "have seen the Lord!" May we, as witnesses of your resurrection, proclaim with Thomas and Mary Magdalene: "My Lord and my God!"

JESUS APPEARS TO TWO ON THE ROAD TO EMMAUS

Liesa Unger (Germany)

LUKE 24:13–35

---

v. 31 *Their eyes were opened and they recognized him.*

Two people—both puzzled and discouraged by the events in their life. As they walk together, they are joined by a stranger. A conversation develops and quickly deepens. They are fascinated, touched, and confused by the words of this stranger, whom they invite to join them for a meal. When the stranger breaks the bread, they suddenly recognize Jesus.

The story is intriguing. Their life is not transformed by the discussion and theological debate they are having, although it seems to be fascinating. Rather, everything changes in the moment when they sit down to eat, the stranger blesses and breaks the bread, and "their eyes were opened" (v. 31). In an instant, they understand that the crucified Jesus is alive, that he has been raised from the dead and is now seated at their table. That moment changes their lives.

This story describes a situation that we have likely all experienced. Life presents us with questions and challenges that we cannot fully grasp or understand. We often have more questions than answers. We are sad, angry, and disappointed, sometimes to the extent that we doubt ourselves and even life itself. We think we are alone and abandoned by God. And yet, at every moment God himself is walking with us. God listens to our questions, our complaints, and our despair. God takes part in the conversation. God gets involved, often without us realizing it.

When Jesus sits down to eat dinner with the two discouraged companions, when he breaks bread with them, they see something that they had previously been blind to. In that ordinary encounter, eating together at the table, they suddenly understand who Jesus is. They become aware of the resurrection, the new life, God's big picture.

There are numerous stories in the Bible about sitting together and sharing meals. Jesus ate with the tax collector, Zacchaeus, he fed the crowd of five thousand, he ate with his disciples and with the teachers of the law. Again and again we read stories about meals. So it is no wonder that his disciples recognize him at the table.

Jesus is interested in our everyday lives. He wants to sit at the table, to eat with us, and to experience fellowship. If we invite Jesus to share the very simple, vital parts of our lives, we will learn who he really is. And, not least, we are likely to recognize Jesus when we sit down at the table with the stranger—when we share what we have and when we open ourselves up to surprising encounters with people outside of our circles.

In my work as event coordinator for Mennonite World Conference (MWC) I have heard many sermons, theological discussions, and teachings about cultural differences. But for me, the real life-changing experiences have happened when I sat down with brothers and sisters from different parts of the world, heard their challenges, experienced their joy, and listened carefully to their perspectives on faith and their responses to the challenges of life. That is the blessing of personal encounters during MWC events. That is when I have learned a great deal about Jesus being alive in people's lives and about God's work in the world.

Sitting down at the table together might be the best way to recognize the presence of Jesus among us.

For reflection

1. When have you experienced a sudden awareness of Jesus' presence in your life?

2. Why is food—table fellowship—such an important theme in the Bible? When have you experienced a profound sense of community around a table?

3. How do you understand this story in relation to the Christian practice of communion or the Lord's Supper?

Prayer

May God bless you and be the light on your path,
    may you feel God's love when you are afraid,
    may God's presence fill your heart with joy,
    may God bless you through people you meet on your way
    and the meals that you share. Amen.

JESUS APPEARS TO THOMAS AND OTHER DISCIPLES

Nelson Martínez Castillo (Colombia)

JOHN 20:24–29

v. 29 *"Do you believe because you see me? Happy are those who don't see and yet believe."*

Who is Jesus to me? I can identify fully with the disciples who walked daily with Jesus, yet often found it hard to believe or understand who Jesus was. I, too, walk with Jesus. And yet I suffer from the same malady as the disciples and find myself asking hard questions every day. Intellectually and theologically, it is clear to me that Jesus is God made flesh and that Jesus came to save me from my sins. But what does this actually mean for me in practice?

Jesus has been relevant throughout my life. I was born in a Christian home in a Latin American country where religion is an important part of life. My parents were pastors, and I had the privilege of serving in the church from a very early age. In my childhood and as a teenager, I was blessed to live a largely quiet life. However, a life free from difficulties and problems often makes it difficult to answer the hard questions with conviction or clarity when things suddenly go wrong.

A couple of years ago, my life took an unexpected turn. My marriage came to an end. And with it came many doubts and much suffering that I never thought I would experience. My thoughts were clouded, and my convictions were shaken in many ways that led me to become very distant from God. Things that once seemed rock solid were now called into question. The language of the Christian life that once seemed so comforting—songs, prayers, claims about God, Jesus, and the Holy Spirit—seemed empty. Suffering and pain can cloud our vision and fill us with doubts, causing us, like Thomas, to demand proof from Jesus.

However, with time, my suffering and sense of distance from God allowed me to arrive at a much clearer conviction of who Jesus is for me. I slowly came to realize that our own suffering and pain will never be greater than the suffering and pain that Jesus experienced out of love for us. As we read in this passage from John 20, his wounds were so real that Thomas could touch them with his own hands.

Being away from God reveals our darkest and dirtiest human side. The greatest tragedy a human being can experience is a life away from the presence of Jesus, a path that leads to death. I have come to understand that we can lose absolutely everything in this life, but that does not mean that we must lose our relationship with Jesus, "our Lord and our God" (v. 28). Following his difficult moment of doubt—after recognizing the actual bodily pain and suffering that Jesus had experienced—Thomas could confess with conviction, "My Lord and my God."

This confession had consequences. If we recognize, as Thomas did, that Jesus is our Lord and our God, we must live in obedience to him, renouncing our way of seeing the world in order to see it through the eyes of Jesus. For me, this was an insight that became real only in the midst of the trials and difficult moments of my life.

Who is Jesus for me? Jesus is a loving Father who always has his arms open to hug and comfort us in the midst of our pain—not only because he understands our pain, but because he lived it in the flesh. Jesus is a merciful and gracious Father who is willing to receive us even when our sin has made us unworthy of his love and forgiveness. Jesus is the only Father capable of transforming and cleansing our lives, so that we can begin to walk in full obedience to him, knowing that he is our Lord and our God.

For reflection

1. Reflect on an unexpected situation that has occurred in your life.

2. What emotions stand out the most when you think about that season?

3. How did these emotions influence your relationship with God at the time?

4. How has your view of God changed as a result of this experience?

Prayer

Dear God, may each person reading this reflection know that they may always bring their burdens, pain, and suffering to the only God and Father capable of understanding the situation they are experiencing. May they always have the certainty that Jesus alone can bring peace in the midst of the difficulties of life. At the same time, may they understand that God wants to transform our lives so that we live according to his will in the midst of a fallen world separated from him. And that they may always remember that a life without God is the greatest tragedy that a human being can experience. Amen.

JESUS COMMISSIONS HIS DISCIPLES TO CONTINUE HIS WORK

Rebeca González Torres (Mexico)

MARK 16:14–18

v. 14 *Finally he appeared to the eleven while they were eating. Jesus criticized their unbelief and stubbornness because they didn't believe those who saw him after he was raised up.*

This passage immediately triggers a question for me: how is Jesus present or relevant on our journey of faith and life?

The question—which needs to be answered by all Christians in all times and places—rings in my mind because I recognize moments in my life when my vulnerability made me hesitate to respond to Jesus' call. The commission that Jesus gives us in this text is to go into the world preaching his message of wholeness and salvation in every circumstance. That call remains a challenge in life.

My husband and I have spent seven years accompanying vulnerable people in both Mexico and the United States who are living in extreme situations—people who are migrating, for example, or family members searching for loved ones who have been "disappeared" by violence. Such people are often experiencing not only the extreme pain of loss but also the existential emptiness that shakes life to the core. There have been moments in those settings when I doubted that Jesus could offer any health or comfort in the face of so much pain.

So it was when the resurrected Jesus appeared to his disciples as they were eating together. His presence was unexpected and extraordinary. The text says that they worshiped him. But at the same time Jesus was deeply frustrated with the disciples because "they didn't believe those who saw him after he was raised up" (v. 14).

I recognize their skepticism. Many times, I have been speechless in the face of extreme pain and profound injustice. Doubts overwhelm me because I often have no answers for what I witness. But I have also received great life lessons from these experiences. I have learned that in times of doubt and uncertainty about the future, my faith can be strengthened and I can affirm that Jesus is truly the way, the truth, and the life—the one who can reanimate hearts and provide renewed energy in the midst of pain.

Recently in the small Mexican city of Cuautla Morelos we met some parents migrating from Honduras with their baby, asking for economic help. On a street corner, a person stopped and gave them a Coke. They opened the soda to transfer it into the baby's bottle. My husband and I immediately rushed to give them money to buy milk or water for their baby. We offered to help them for a few days, told them about the difficult situation at the border, and warned them about the various difficulties they would likely encounter on the way. In the end, they decided to continue on their way, pulled against all odds by a dream they wanted to fulfill. Migrants who have decided to leave extremely difficult circumstances to seek new life opportunities are often willing to endure any hardships they encounter along the way.

The same is true of people searching for their missing family members. I remember a mother telling me that if the evildoers plan their misdeeds and organize themselves to carry out their evil intentions, why don't we as a society also organize ourselves to take care of each other or collectively strategize to prevent these tragedies that destroy the tranquility of families?

Those words led me to affirm the importance of walking like Jesus, obeying his instructions to preach the good news of salvation and to invite others into the presence of the Risen One who gives hope to all.

For me, this is the answer to this question of how to make Jesus present in the journey of faith and life. Jesus becomes alive when we accompany the vulnerable, the marginalized, and the needy. The guarantee of his resurrection is the assurance he gives us as we share the good news of health, salvation, and peace with everyone who desires a new life. So in all circumstances, I can say with great conviction that sharing the good news of Jesus, who is the Savior, brings peace to all people of good will.

For reflection

1. In what circumstances in life have you doubted?

2. How do you reaffirm that Jesus is the Savior?

3. What actions do you take when you see the pain of a migrant or a family who cannot find their missing loved ones?

Prayer

Father, full of goodness, you who know the pain of the human condition—we ask your protection for all people who have lost all their resources and are looking for other opportunities in life. We ask for your guidance and wisdom to help them achieve stability. Open the hands and hearts of your church so that your goodness will extend to them at all times and in all places.

We also pray for the children and young people who are victims of organized crime and are abducted by evildoers. May you be their consolation and protection. We pray for the church to be a place of refuge and community organization that offers security and mutual aid. Guide our decisions and protect us so that we may see the miracles brought about by Jesus, the Risen One. Amen.

Part 8

NEW LIFE

Walking in the Resurrection

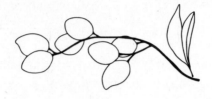

JESUS PROCLAIMS GOOD NEWS TO THE POOR

Carlos Martínez-García (Mexico)

LUKE 4:14–22

v. 18 *"He has sent me to preach good news to the poor, to proclaim release to the prisoners and recovery of sight to the blind, to liberate the oppressed."*

In the first century and in the twenty-first century there is hopeful news for the dispossessed and oppressed. In the first-century world where Jesus ministered, the majority of the population suffered from the political, economic, and religious domination of local and foreign elites. Today, global powers, with the complicity of national partners, keep in poverty millions of people who see no way out of conditions of daily life that they do not deserve.

The words that Jesus reads from the prophet Isaiah—including his claim that the hope of liberation was being fulfilled by the one doing the reading—should make us reflect on one of the programmatic points of the gospel that Jesus embodied and its repercussions for those of us who intend to follow in his footsteps. These verses do not exhaust the essential message of the gospel, but they are a basic part of the total liberation that Jesus imagined for human beings.

Luke emphasizes that it was "the power of the Spirit" that brought Jesus back to Galilee (v. 14). He remained in the region for a significant amount of time, long enough to teach in several synagogues (v. 15). His teaching made him known in various Galilean towns. In Jesus' time, Galilee had 204 towns. Even though he did not visit all, or even most, of them, according to Luke's narrative he was present in several and, as a result, he was "praised by everyone." Those who heard his teachings in the synagogues also admired him (v. 15). Later Luke gives more space to narrate what happened in a specific town in Galilee, Nazareth, where Jesus had grown up (v. 16).

Luke depicts Jesus teaching among all kinds of people and in all kinds of contexts, whether at a table or in conversations on the road. In this passage, he relates that Jesus would attend a synagogue on the Sabbath, which he does while in Nazareth. The liturgy in the synagogue included two readings, one from the Law and one from the Prophets. In Nazareth, Jesus stood up and read from the scroll of the prophet Isaiah (Isaiah 61:1–2). The same Spirit that brought Jesus to Galilee is the one who, according to the prophet, chooses and anoints the one who brings the message of liberation. The liberation proclaimed here is economic—it restores people from the wounds caused by poverty. The deliverance reaches the enslaved, those who have been taken against their will far from their homelands and are forced to submit to the will of those who uprooted them. The promised deliverance frees people from the blindness caused by abusive conditions imposed on them. The liberation announced by Isaiah, and renewed by Jesus, breaks the chains of all forms of oppression that are contrary to God's purpose for humanity (v. 18–19).

In the synagogue it was customary for the reader to explain the section that the audience had just heard. This was to happen when the reader sat down, teaching from the chair (*ex cathedra*). Those present in the synagogue fixed their eyes on Jesus (v. 20), awaiting the words of the one whose fame had spread throughout Galilee. Jesus did not offer a detailed exposition of the passage. Instead, he simply affirmed in a few short words that he was the one who incarnated the promise announced by the prophet (v. 21). Luke notes that the listeners accepted Jesus' affirmation, "impressed . . . by the gracious words flowing from his lips" (v. 22). How can we reconcile this claim by Jesus with his origins, which were not prestigious? Was he not the son of a simple worker? Nor could he claim credentials from learning at the feet of some well-known rabbi. The answer is implied by Luke in the narrative—it was the Spirit who acted in Jesus (v. 14); and, at the same time, Jesus incarnated the Spirit.

I am originally from Mexico City, an enormous metropolis. Some experts say it is the most populated city in the world. I have enjoyed its rich cultural offerings and the diversity of its inhabitants. Several years ago, however, my ministerial environment and activities suddenly changed. I began to travel frequently to Chiapas, a region with the largest and most ethnically-diverse indigenous population: Tzotziles, Tzeltales, Choles, Tojolabales, Mames, Zoques, Lacandones, and others. I met and lived very closely with many converts to Christianity, men and women alike, who had suffered cruel persecution for breaking with traditional religious practices and the dominant territorial churches.

Among the persecuted were a large number of martyrs, cruelly killed. Like the Anabaptists in the sixteenth century, those who survived were forced to emigrate to different parts of Chiapas where, amid very precarious material conditions, they were forced to build new homes. The people of Chiapas taught me to understand more deeply and more fully that the gospel offers the good news of liberation from poverty and oppression. In indigenous culture, spiritual and material goods are inseparable. The gospel of Jesus breaks all the chains that bind one's personal life. But it also, according to my indigenous brothers and sisters, should incite Christians to transform unjust structures in society.

Could it be that they have a better understanding and practice of the liberating message of Jesus?

For reflection

1. How does Jesus challenge us, personally and communally, to incarnate the end of all forms of oppression?

2. Are we aware that Jesus made his liberating proclamation in Galilee from below, stripped of political and economic power? What would it mean to follow him in that same path?

3. What living examples ("living letters," according to Paul in 2 Corinthians 3:2–4) do we bring to heart and mind that might encourage us to work for a life of dignity for all people?

Prayer

May the same Spirit that mobilized Jesus to go throughout Galilee also compel us to proclaim and live the good news of total liberation. Strengthen us to work daily for the kingdom principles of the gospel in our settings, without losing sight of the global dimensions that often reinforce the chains that oppress. Thank you, Lord, for those from the margins of society, without resources that grant prestige and power, who serve as living signs, sowing the good news of spiritual and material freedom that the prophet Isaiah envisioned and that Jesus incarnated. May the Holy Spirit give us hope, and the strength to avoid the temptation of the despair that blinds us. Let us be grateful that the Spirit gives us the gift of seeing reality in a new way. Amen.

JESUS GIVES THE GREATEST COMMANDMENT

Mollee Moua (Canada)

JOHN 15:9–17

---

vv. 12–13 *"This is my commandment: love each other just as I have loved you. No one has greater love than to give up one's life for one's friends."*

In the 1960s and 1970s many Hmong families fled from Laos to Thailand to avoid the new communist regime. During the Vietnam War, the Hmong people had fought alongside the United States against the Communist forces. So when the US lost the war, the Hmong were persecuted and forced to flee as refugees. In April 1978 my mother and my father were among those who crossed the Mekong River under the cover of darkness. My mother carried my oldest brother, who was only a few months old, on her back as she moved fearfully and silently through the jungle.

Traveling with a baby was dangerous, especially because their frequent cries attracted unwanted attention. One night, my mother cut her foot badly on some bamboo while walking in the dark. It was nothing short of a miracle that they arrived safely at a refugee camp where they would be sponsored by a Mennonite congregation and, in June 1980, arrive in Canada.

As mothers, we make many sacrifices for our children. I can only imagine the strength and bravery my mother and father needed during that treacherous journey. But they did what had to be done to survive and to provide a better future for their family. In fact, as caregivers many of us often prioritize the needs of those we love over our own. We perform the duties necessary to ensure that our children receive the care, support, and nourishment that they need.

After I became a mother, everything about my physical, mental, and spiritual self completely changed. There was a part of me living in another human being. This gift of life was a decision that would impact me forever. I imagine that when God became flesh in Jesus, all the sacrifices God chose to make required no second thought.

As the mother of four young boys, I feel like the to-do list is never ending. Yet whether it's laundry, cooking, helping with homework, or repeatedly answering the same questions, we somehow find the time for it all. Sure, there are moments when we need rest and time to recharge. But at the end of the day when I look around and see dried tips on the markers (after repeatedly reminding them to put the lids back on), I also often encounter a drawing that brings warmth to my heart. I do what I need to do each day because those are the tasks of a good mother.

To me, Jesus is a mother. In the text for today, Jesus tells the disciples, "As the Father has loved me, so I have loved you" (John 15:9 NRSVue). Throughout his time with his disciples, Jesus mentored, loved, and provided for his disciples. He took time to teach and instruct them separately when they didn't understand his teachings. His love was unconditional. He took care of his disciples . . . and he continues to take care of his followers today.

Jesus has been with me and my family all the way from Laos to Canada. Indeed, he was present there long before that time. He lifted us out of physical and spiritual poverty into prosperity. But it doesn't end there. Jesus commanded us to love each other—to love the least of these, to love our enemies. He continues to challenge me every day, inviting me to extend that same love to all those I encounter.

For reflection

1. Consider the statement, "After I became a mother, everything about my physical, mental, and spiritual self completely changed." How have major life changes impacted your relationship with God and others?

2. Reflect on the idea of unconditional love as demonstrated by Jesus. How can you embody this kind of love in your daily interactions?

3. What sacrifices have you made in your own life for the benefit of others, and how have these sacrifices shaped your identity and purpose?

4. Reflect on a time when you felt overwhelmed by your responsibilities. How did you find the strength to continue, and what did you learn from that experience?

5. How do you relate to the idea of Jesus being like a mother? In what ways does this perspective change or deepen your understanding of Jesus' role in your life?

Prayer

Jesus,

You birthed me like my earthly mother—your cry on the cross gave me abundant life. I am your child needing instruction and encouragement. I am eager to serve. Give me the courage to face the sacrifices before me. May we choose each day to shower in your love. Help us to love each other as you have loved us. Amen.

WHO DO YOU SAY THAT I AM?

Siaka Traoré (Burkina Faso)

MATTHEW 16:13–20

v. 16 *"You are the Christ, the Son of the living God."*

As Jesus nears the end of his ministry, he carries out a self-evaluation. Politicians today frequently conduct surveys to get a sense of what the people think of them. Jesus' self-evaluation proceeds in two stages. In the first, he asks about the general opinion of society, "Who do people say that I, the Son of Man, am?" (Matthew 16:13 NKJV, here and following). Society's opinion of Jesus was positive. No criticism. People even compared him to other important figures in the Bible.

In the second part of the survey, he turned to his immediate disciples, those who were with him night and day, who had witnessed his moods and perspectives. To them, he asked: "But who do you say that I am?" It was Peter who gave the most beautiful response to the question—indeed the most beautiful insight he had ever made: "You are the Christ, the Son of the living God." Jesus affirmed that this answer came from God his Father.

The question Jesus asked of the disciples some two thousand years ago remains relevant for the disciples of all generations, especially ours. Jesus' question leads me to ask myself: What mark has he left on my life? Today, the question might be: What do people think of me? What do people in the church and in society see in my daily life?

Jesus is no longer here among us, but he is indeed alive in those who have received him and believed in him: "I have been crucified with Christ and I no longer live, but Christ lives in me. And the life that I now live in my body, I live by faith, indeed, by the faithfulness of God's Son, who loved me and gave himself for me." (Galatians 2:20).

Because Christ is no longer physically present among us, he must be seen today through my life as his disciple. This representation of Jesus Christ that I reflect must affect all areas of my life.

Who is Jesus in my family life? Do my wife and children see me as a model of Jesus? When I talk about Jesus, am I representing what Jesus said and did? As a pastor, if I do not embody the moral and spiritual values that identify me with Jesus Christ, it would be difficult for me to ask others to live according to the model of Jesus.

I recall an encounter with a pastor during my training in Bible school. Through an explanation in a class on the nature of sin, this man came face-to-face with his true character—the sin that was revealed in his behavior. This recognition upset him so much that he began to cry. No one in the class could console him, and at one point the whole class joined him in his tears. When he returned home with swollen eyes, his wife asked him who beat him so badly that he cried so hard. The man asked his wife to leave the family courtyard and accompany him to a quiet place. There he asked her, "What kind of husband do you think I am?" The woman bluntly replied, "You are the meanest husband, the worst man, I have ever met." Again he began to cry, saying to his wife, "So this is what you really think of me?"

How many of us are willing to ask our wives or children what they honestly think of us? But even if you don't do that, every follower of Jesus Christ must ask themselves the same question.

How are we to be salt and light in an increasingly corrupt world? God gives us the opportunity to recognize the difference between his children of light and those who live according to the way of this world. Our life as disciples of Christ must be shaped by a Christian ethic supported by the wisdom of the Holy Spirit.

Several years ago, I bought a piece of land in Ouagadougou, the capital city of Burkina Faso. In order to transfer the documents in my name I had to pay taxes. The lady who had to calculate the fees to be paid told me: "Pastor, if you declare the exact amount of the purchase of the land, you will pay more taxes. You really should report a lower amount." I replied that I preferred to declare the exact amount. That way, if there is a legal dispute someday in the future, I will be able to say exactly what I paid.

For reflection

1. Imagine that Jesus is before you asking the same question he asked his disciples, "Who do people say that I, the Son of Man, am?"

2. Reflect on how you would answer the question personally. "Who do *you* say that I am?"

3. What are the implications of recognizing Jesus as "the Christ, the Son of the living God" in your daily life?

Prayer

"Examine me, God! Look at my heart! Put me to the test! Know my anxious thoughts! Look to see if there is any idolatrous way in me, then lead me on the eternal path!" (Psalm 139:23–24).

JESUS SENDS OUT HIS DISCIPLES TO PREACH AND HEAL

John Wambura (Tanzania)

LUKE 9:1–6

---

v. 3 *"Take nothing for the journey—no walking stick, no bag, no bread, no money, not even an extra shirt."*

In this text from the gospel of Luke, Jesus calls the twelve disciples together and gives them power and authority over all demons and to cure diseases. He sends them out to proclaim the kingdom of God and to heal the sick. He instructs them to take nothing for their journey—no staff, no bag, no bread, no money, and no extra shirt. They are to rely entirely on God's provision and the hospitality of those they encounter.

Reflecting on this passage, I am reminded of the profound impact of Jesus' commission on my own life. Growing up in the rural area of Bukiroba, Tanzania, and later working with international organizations like the United Nations World Food Programme and the Center for Disease Control (CDC)–US Embassy in Dar es Salaam, I have experienced the living presence of Jesus in various cultural contexts. Jesus' call to preach, heal, and serve resonates deeply with my professional journey and personal faith.

In 2008, I was called to leave my employment at CDC where my salary was about $1,900 per month, to join the Mennonite Church as a full-time pastor and diocesan secretary at a paycheck of $100 per month. At that time, I was married with five children. That was the first time my faith was seriously challenged, and I experienced complete dependence on God, almost in the sense of Jesus instructing disciples to "take nothing for the journey" (Luke 9:3).

In my daily life as a pastor, Jesus is not only a spiritual guide but also a model of compassionate leadership and selfless service. His instructions to the disciples to rely on God and the hospitality of others remind me of the importance of humility and trust in God's provision. Whether coordinating food distribution in refugee camps or facilitating women and youth economic empowerment programs, I have seen God's hand at work in the kindness and generosity of the people I encounter.

In 2013, I was sent to minister to a very poor community in Nyantira, Kitunda, Dar es Salaam. The congregation was too small to pay a salary. Yet God gave me vocational opportunities around the community and a house to live in rent-free until I was able to raise enough money to cover the house rent.

In my local congregations at Nyantira (2013–2022) and Upanga (2023 to present), the teachings of Jesus have inspired us to engage in community services and outreach. Much like the disciples did, we strive to embody the values of compassion, humility, and reliance on God. This passage challenges us to step out in faith, trusting that God will provide and guide us as we serve others. I have experienced

God's power made visible during services to deliver his people from bondage, casting out demonic forces, and destroying the spirits of poverty, sicknesses, and ancestral diseases.

I have also witnessed the physical and spiritual growth of the church (his kingdom) at both congregations. The number of young leaders and cell groups have multiplied and church members have begun to express a deeper sense of hospitality.

Throughout my life and ministry in Tanzania, I have witnessed the vibrant faith and resilience of the local communities. The cultural context here is rich with communal values, where people support one another in times of need. This sense of community aligns with Jesus' instructions to his disciples to depend on the hospitality of others. In my work with international organizations and the Mennonite church, I have seen this communal spirit play a crucial role in various programs and initiatives. For example, we have been receiving students from Goshen College (Indiana) through their Study Service-Term who live for a period of time with host families from our congregations. For the students, this is one expression of what it means to depend on God to provide a home and trustworthy relationships for students in a foreign setting. But it also has enabled host families to receive a student sent by God to their homes, so that strangers can become friends with Jesus at the center.

For reflection

1. How can we cultivate a deeper sense of dependence on God in our daily lives?

2. What practical steps can we take to embody the values of compassion and humility in our communities?

3. How can we encourage a culture of hospitality and generosity in our local congregations and beyond?

Prayer

Heavenly Father, we thank you for the gift of your Son, Jesus Christ, who calls us to follow him in love and service. As we reflect on his teachings and his commission to the disciples, we ask for the courage and faith to step out in trust and obedience. Fill our hearts with compassion and humility, and guide our steps as we serve others in your name.

Lord, bless our communities with the spirit of hospitality and generosity. May we always be mindful of the needs of those around us, and may we find joy in giving and receiving support. Strengthen our faith and help us to rely on your provision in all circumstances. In Jesus' name, we pray. Amen.

THE GREAT COMMISSION

Agus W. Mayanto (Indonesia)

MATTHEW 28:16–20

---

vv. 19–20 *"Therefore, go and make disciples of all nations, baptizing them in the name of the Father and of the Son and of the Holy Spirit, teaching them to obey everything that I've commanded you."*

I am a Javanese living in Indonesia. In our culture, the peak of the spiritual journey is an achievement called *manunggaling kawula lan Gusti*, or a "union with the Lord God, the Creator and Source of Life." This is where a harmonious life and peaceful order occurs that unites the *jagad cilik* (lit. "small world"), or oneself, with the *jagad gedhe* (lit. "big world), or the universe of living space. In this union, both worlds are in a harmonious relationship even though the dynamics of both are different and not always in sync. Nevertheless, a harmony is well-maintained.

The peak of the spiritual journey is achieved through the path of *ngelmu*—a tireless study to gain knowledge of life as if it were a search to find the "nest of the wind" (*susuhing angin*) or the "footprints of a bird in flight" (*tapak Kuntul mabur*). This pilgrimage may seem impossible but is still carried out with sincerity, because the key to spirituality is not only to be found in achievement but in perseverance and intentionality in each step of the pilgrimage journey. The path of *ngelmu* can be successful only if the disciple (*santri*) has a worthy, qualified teacher (*guru*). By living together in full obedience to the *guru*, the *santri* absorbs his knowledge, breathes his spirit, listens to his teachings, and follows his example. So the path of discipleship is a pilgrimage of faith that leads the disciple to an experience of unity with the Lord God the Creator and Source of Life.

The mandate of the Lord Jesus to his disciples is very relevant to this pilgrimage of faith, especially because it was conveyed by Christ, the true Lord and Master, and by God who has power and authority over earth and heaven (Matthew 28:18). In this passage, Jesus—who, as the Lord Great Teacher holds knowledge and has power over everything—gives a mandate that should be followed and carried out by his disciples, because it is the living word of the true, honest, and just ruler, which is to be emulated and followed (*Sabda Pandhita Ratu*). Jesus the Teacher, who is God, not only speaks to us, but has transcended the distance of space and the time of eternity, has entered into the world of death, and triumphed over it—a reality confirmed by the resurrection.

"Go and make disciples of all nations" is the mandate to bring the Lord Teacher's invitation to all people, regardless of geographical boundaries, ethnicity, skin color, economic class, or social status—indeed, to all human beings, who are equal before him. This great commission conveys an invitation in a peaceful manner, without violence or coercion, because what is expected is a conscious response and a voluntary decision to believe and follow Jesus. The decision to consciously and voluntarily become a disciple of Jesus, the Master Teacher, is an important foundation for baptism. It is a commitment to bind oneself with the Triune God, the missionary God who in the incarnation brings reconciliation and union with all creation (or *manunggaling kawula lan Gusti*—the union of the servant/creation with the Master Creator and the Source of Life).

This decision to bind oneself with the missionary God—the Creator, Savior, and Sustainer who reconciles the entire universe with himself—is also the path of discipleship, walking in the way of the Master Teacher Jesus in the midst of the world in full obedience, attentive to his voice, moved by his Spirit, and following his example. The sixteenth-century Anabaptist Hans Denck once said, "No one can truly know Christ unless he follows him daily in life." Therefore, in the process of discipleship, we must heed the words of the Master Teacher Christ, "teaching them to obey everything that I've commanded you" (Matthew 28:20). It is impossible to be a disciple of Christ without a commitment to live in harmony with his will.

For reflection

1. How have you experienced communion and union with God, the Creator and Source of Life?

2. How is the path of discipleship also a spiritual pilgrimage?

3. What approach to "making disciples" is most relevant for this generation in your context?

Prayer

O Christ—Lord, Grand Master, and Teacher. We are grateful that you have reconciled us with the Creator, the source of our life, so that we have life and hope. Help us to be sensitive to your invitation to become believers and to live as your disciples. May the Holy Spirit guide us to persevere every day in following you and obeying all your commandments so that one day we can be in complete unity with you, the Creator and Source of Life. Amen.

THE CONTRIBUTORS

Desalegn Abebe is a pastor and the president of the Meserete Kristos Church in Ethiopia. He also serves as a member of MWC Faith and Life Commission.

Cindy Alpízar is a pastor at the Iglesia Menonita Jesucristo es el Señor in Heredia, Costa Rica, and a member of the National Council of the Mennonite Conference of Costa Rica. She also serves as president of Seminario Semilla in Guatemala, as co-coordinator of the Anabaptist Women's Movement Doing Theology in Latin America, and in various projects related to the work of Mennonite World Conference.

Kkot-Ip Bae, from Nonsan-si, South Korea, is a member of the MWC Young Anabaptists (YABs) committee.

Neal Blough was previously co-director of the Paris Mennonite Centre in France and professor of church history at the Faculté Libre de Théologie Evangélique. He is a member of the Châtenay-Malabry Mennonite congregation and of the MWC Peace Commission.

Jürg Bräker serves as the general secretary for the Swiss Mennonite Conference and is part of the leadership in the Mennonite congregation in Bern, Switzerland. He has served on the MWC Deacons Commission and is currently a member of the MWC Executive Committee.

Lisa Carr-Pries is the vice-president of Mennonite World Conference, and a member of Mennonite Church Canada. She works as the Director of Spiritual Care at Parkwood Mennonite Seniors Community in Waterloo, Ontario, Canada.

Jeremiah Choi, a voluntary pastor of the Agape Mennonite Church in Hong Kong, is the MWC regional representative for Northeast Asia.

Linda Dibble has been the moderator of Mennonite Church USA and is currently a member of the MWC Executive Committee. She is a member of the Albany Mennonite Church, Albany, Oregon, USA.

Gracia Felo is a young leader in the Community of Mennonite Brethren Churches in Congo (CEFMC), where he serves as chorister and vice-president of youth in the local church in Kikwit, Democratic Republic of the Congo. He is a delegate to the MWC General Council and a member of the MWC Mission Commission.

Rebeca González Torres has been a pastor in Mennonite churches in Mexico City, Mexico, and various other countries in the Spanish-speaking world for thirty-five years. Along the way, she has served in numerous ministries related to service, peacemaking, and accompaniment, focusing especially on migrants and support for relatives of victims of political violence. She is an active participant in the Movement of Anabaptist Women Doing Theology in Latin America and is a member of the MWC Faith and Life Commission.

Anne-Cathy Graber is a Franco-Swiss pastor and theologian who lives as a religious sister in the Chemin Neuf ecumenical community. A member of the Mennonite congregation in Châtenay-Malabry, France, she is co-director of the Chair of Ecumenical Theology at the Loyola Faculties in Paris, France (Jesuit Faculties), and a member of the MWC Faith and Life Commission. She also represents MWC on several international ecumenical commissions.

Barbara Hege-Galle has been executive secretary of the Mennonite Voluntary Service program in Germany (Christliche Dienste) for thirty-two years. She currently serves on the leadership team of her local congregation in Bammental, Germany, and as second chair of the Mennonite Youth Ministries in southern Germany. She also serves on the MWC Mission Commission and as chair of the Global Anabaptist Service Network (GASN).

Atsuhiro Katano, a member of the Sapporo Bethel Mennonite Church in Japan, helps to manage the Fukuzumi Mennonite Center in Sapporo, Japan, and serves as an organizer of Northeast Asia Regional Peacebuilding Institute and the Christian Forum for Reconciliation in Northeast Asia. He is a member of the MWC Faith and Life Commission.

Doug Klassen, from Calgary, Alberta, Canada, served as a pastor for twenty-eight years in three Mennonite Church Canada congregations before being called to serve as executive minister in 2019. In 2022 he was selected to serve on the MWC Executive Committee.

Reinhard Kummer is a member of the board of the Mennonite Free Church of Austria and a member of the MWC Deacons Commission.

Valentina Kunze is a youth leader in the Conference of Mennonite Churches in Uruguay and is the MWC Young Anabaptists (YABs) representative for Latin America.

Sunoko Lin, from Lake Balboa, California, USA, is a senior pastor of Maranatha Christian Fellowship and serves as the treasurer of Mennonite World Conference.

Nelson Martínez Castillo, from Bogotá, Colombia, serves on the MWC staff as an administrative assistant. He is an active member of Nuevo Amanecer, a Mennonite Brethren church in Colombia, where he contributes to the worship and young adult ministry.

Carlos Martínez-García is a sociologist and journalist who also serves as an Anabaptist-Mennonite pastor in Mexico City, Mexico, and is director of the Anabaptist Studies Center there. The author of numerous articles and books, he is a member of the MWC Executive Committee.

Nelson Martínez Muñoz is lead pastor of Nuevo Amanecer, a Mennonite Brethren congregation in Bogotá, Colombia.

Agus W. Mayanto is a pastor of the GKMI Cempaka Putih congregation in Jakarta, Indonesia, chair of the GKMI Synod in Indonesia, and a Southeast Asia Regional Representative for Mennonite World Conference.

Mollee Moua is managing editor for Anabaptism at 500, an initiative of MennoMedia, and attends First Hmong Mennonite Church in Kitchener, Ontario, Canada.

Sindah Ngulube is a bishop of the Brethren In Christ Church in Zimbabwe and a member of the MWC Executive Committee. He and his wife Suzen are the parents of two adult daughters.

Nelson Okanya was born and raised in Kenya. A former pastor and president of Eastern Mennonite Missions, he currently serves as president of World Serving Leaders, the nonprofit division of the Center for Serving Leadership, and as chair of the Global Mission Fellowship, serving seventy-one member organizations through Mennonite World Conference.

Samson Omondi Ongode is the presiding moderator bishop of the Kenya Mennonite Church and a member of the MWC Executive Committee.

Sue Park-Hur is an ordained minister and director of racial ethnic engagement for Mennonite Church USA. She is also a co-founder of ReconciliAsian and a member of MWC Deacons Commission.

Cynthia (Margaret) Peacock, of Kolkata, India, has served as MWC South Asia Regional Representative (India and Nepal) since 2015. She is a member of the Tollygunje Christian Fellowship, under BJCPM (Bharatiya Jukta Christa Prochar Mandali/India United Missionary Church), where she is an elder. Peacock served with Mennonite Central Committee in India on the board of the Mennonite Christian Service Fellowship of India for nearly four decades.

Willi Hugo Pérez is the academic dean of the Latin American Anabaptist Seminary (SEMILLA) in Guatemala City, Guatemala, and the MWC regional representative for Central America.

Felix Perez Diener, from Las Vegas, Nevada, USA, is a member of the MWC Young Anabaptists (YABs) committee.

Preshit Rao is the information technology coordinator of Mennonite World Conference, the advisor of his local youth group, and a member of the audio and visual team at the Mennonite Church of Rajnandgaon, India.

Vikal Pravin Rao is a member of the Mennonite Church, Rajnandgaon, India. He also serves as executive secretary of the Mennonite Church in India (Chhattisgarh, India), treasurer of the Mennonite Christian Service Fellowship of India, and as a member of the MWC Deacons Commission.

Henk Stenvers is president of Mennonite World Conference and a member of the Doopsgezinde Gemeente in Bussum-Naarden, Netherlands. In 2020 he retired from his position as general secretary of the Dutch Mennonite Conference (Algemene Doopsgezinde Sociëteit).

Hyacinth Stevens has served the church as a pastor, bishop, teacher, mentor, and program developer. She is currently serving as the executive director of MCC East Coast (USA) and is a member of the MWC Mission Commission.

Tigist Tesfaye Gelagle is secretary of the MWC Deacons Commission and a member of the Meserete Kristos Church in Addis Ababa, Ethiopia.

Kari Traoré is a pastor of the Église Evangélique Mennonite du Burkina Faso, a member of the MWC Peace Commission, and a delegate from Burkina Faso to the MWC General Council.

Siaka Traoré is a pastor with the Église Evangélique Mennonite du Burkina Faso. Currently, he also serves as the MWC regional representative for Central and West Africa.

Liesa Unger is the international events coordinator for Mennonite World Conference. She lives in Frankenthal, Germany, where she is a member of Kohlhof Mennonite Church.

Wieteke van der Molen is pastor and director of Dopersduin, a Mennonite Broederschapshuis, or retreat center, in Schoorl, Netherlands. She serves as a member of the MWC Executive Committee.

John Wambura is a pastor at Upanga Mennonite Church in Dar es Salaam, Tanzania, assistant to the bishop of the Eastern Diocese of the Mennonite Church of Tanzania, executive director of Equip for Change NGO, and a member of the Steering Committee of the Global Anabaptist Peace Network (GAPN) of the Mennonite World Conference.

Rafael Zaracho is a member of Cristiana de la Paz, a Mennonite Brethren congregation in Asunción, Paraguay, and the academic dean of the Instituto Bíblico Asunción (IBA). Zaracho also serves as secretary of the MWC Mission Commission.

NOTES

1. https://commons.wikimedia.org/wiki/File:Matthias_Gr%C3%BCnewald_-_The_Crucifixion_ (detail)_-_WGA10726.jpg.
2. Barbara A. Holmes, "Good and Necessary Anger," Richard Rohr's Daily Meditations, the Center for Action and Contemplation, Feb. 26, 2024, https://cac.org.
3. Richard Rohr, "Jesus' Anger," Richard Rohr's Daily Meditations, the Center for Action and Contemplation, Feb. 25, 2024, https://cac.org.
4. Frederick W. Danker, *Jesus and the New Age: A Commentary on St Luke's Gospel* (Philadelphia: Fortress Press, 1988), 348.
5. The Filipino artist Joey Velasco beautifully captures how the wounded hands and side of Christ are clear signs of God's love for us and others. Start by holding Caravaggio's painting of Thomas in your mind. Then spend some time with Velasco's "A Table of Hope" ("Hapag ng pag asa") followed by "In Thy Wounds" (2006). Available at https://joeyvelascofoundation.wordpress.com/joeys-paintings/.

THE EDITOR

John D. Roth is project director of MennoMedia's Anabaptism at 500 initiative. Prior to that role, Roth was a professor of history at Goshen College (1985–2022), where he also served as director of the Mennonite Historical Library and editor of the *Mennonite Quarterly Review*. Roth has published widely on topics related to Anabaptist-Mennonite history, theology, and church life. He is also the founding director of the Institute for the Study of Global Anabaptism at Goshen College and is active in Mennonite World Conference. John and his wife Ruth enjoy spending time with their grandchildren and are members of Berkey Avenue Mennonite Fellowship in Goshen, Indiana.